PATAGONIA

At the Bottom of the World

Dick Lutz

Dimi Press

Other books by Dick Lutz:

HIDDEN AMAZON

KOMODO, THE LIVING DRAGON with J.
Marie Lutz

THE RUNNING INDIANS

FEEL BETTER! LIVE LONGER! RELAX!

PATAGONIA

At the Bottom of the World

Dick Lutz

DIMI PRESS   Salem, Oregon

DIMI PRESS
3820 Oak Hollow Lane, SE
Salem, Oregon 97302-4774

© 2002 by Dick Lutz

Publisher's Cataloging-In-Publication
       (by Kari Martinez)
Lutz, Richard L.
    Patagonia: at the bottom of the world/Dick
                                         Lutz
       p. ; cm.
       ISBN: 0-931625-38-6
       1. Patagonia (Argentina and Chile) –
       Description and travel 2. Patagonia
       (Argentina and Chile) – History 3.
       Natural history – Patagonia (Ar-
       gentina and Chile) I. Title.

       918.2'7—dc21

Library of Congress Control Number:
                                   2002090633

Cover by Bruce DeRoos

12 pt. Palatino

To my wife, Mary, with many thanks

for her steadfast help with this book.

ACKNOWLEDGEMENTS

This book could not have been written without the assistance of Scott Jones, Buzz Peavy, Russ Grimes, Andrew Haffenden, Veronica Rhoads, and the other helpful folks at International Expeditions.

The most useful person during my research was Miriam Johnson of the Salem Public Library, Salem, Oregon. Also my thanks are due to the Oregon State University Library, Corvallis, Oregon; the Willamette University Library, Salem, Oregon; the Linfield College Library, McMinnville, Oregon; Greater Victoria Public Library, Victoria, British Columbia, Canada; and the Library of Congress, Washington, DC.

The poet, Mary Jo Eisenach, graciously gave permission to use her poem, PATAGONIA.

South America

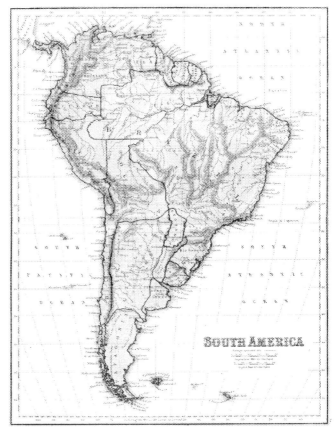

Patagonia is located at the southern tip.

INTRODUCTION

Patagonia is a region, not a country. It spans the southern third of Chile and Argentina, stretching between the Pacific and the Atlantic roughly from Puerto Montt, Chile and Peninsula Valdes, Argentina south till it meets the famous waterways of the Strait of Magellan, Beagle Channel, and Drake Passage (or Drake Strait). The northern limit of Patagonia is ill-defined, while the border between Chile and Argentina divides the region.

Patagonia makes up about a third of the land area of Argentina and Chile, yet only about five percent of the people of those countries live there. Nonetheless, Patagonia is a land of incredible diversity. On the Chilean side, the soaring Andes, inland fjords, rich forests, and small towns dominate; on the Argentine side, huge distances and barren expanses prevail.

But the true Patagonia is farther south, encompassing the tip of the continent. This is the Patagonia most often described as wind-swept, sparsely populated, remote, and rugged. It is rich in wildlife and human history, sprinkled with sheep *estancias* (ranches) and punctuated by national parks, towering snowcapped mountains, glistening glaciers, and deep blue fjords and bays. In some areas, wide sweeping vistas of steppes are evident as far as the naked eye can see.

One indication of the low population is that one of the twentieth century's largest volcanic eruptions occurred in the far north of Patagonia in August 1991 and almost no one noticed. Hundreds of thousands of sheep were killed but no people. This was an eruption of the Hudson volcano, which was far larger than Mt. St. Helens in 1980. Another volcano, the Maca, is in an even more remote area of northern Patagonia and is even less studied. Patagonia is not only sparsely populated and under explored but even its name has generated controversy.

There are at least three theories for where the name *Patagonia* originates. The one preferred by the Oxford English Dictionary is that it comes from the Spanish word *patagon* meaning a large clumsy foot. Magellan, the first foreign visitor to the land below, remarked on the depth of the footprints the dancing natives made in the sand. But other writers have maintained that *patagon* is not really a Spanish word at all.

A second, and I think unlikely, theory is that the Incas, who lived much farther north on the South American continent had a word in their Quechua language *Patac-Hunia* meaning mountain regions. Since Spanish does not pronounce the *h* the word sounds much like Patagonia. However, there are at least two flaws in the argument for this derivation. One, how the Quechua pronunciation came to be said in Spanish is not explained, and two, why would the

Incas who lived in the high Andes describe the much lower Patagonian mountains as mountain regions?

The third theory speculates that Magellan, the man who named Patagonia, did so because some of the Indians of the area (the Tehuelches) wore dog-faced masks. A popular novel of Magellan's time, *Primaleon of Greece*, featured a dog-faced monster named Patagon. It is likely that Magellan had read this book. The anonymous romance was published in Spain in 1512 and translated into English by Anthony Mundy in 1596. Mundy was a friend of William Shakespeare who wrote *The Tempest*. In this famous play Trinculo says of Caliban, "I shall laugh myself to death at this puppy-headed monster."

It seems unlikely that a geographical area would be named after a character in a novel, and yet the state of California was named after an island in *The Adventures of Esplandian*, written by Garci Ordoñez de Montalvo in 1510.

In addition to the many interesting facts about Patagonia brought to light in this book one other deserves mention here. That is the frequent reference to it in literature. Patagonia is a relatively isolated, underpopulated, and barren part of the world suffering from poor weather conditions. One wouldn't expect that such a place would appear very often in literature.

Therefore it may come as a surprise that such giants of literature as Shakespeare, Lord Byron,

Jules Verne, Herman Melville, Arthur Conan Doyle, Edgar Allen Poe, and others have referred to something in Patagonia or written directly about it. The famous poem by Samuel Taylor Coleridge, *The Rime of the Ancient Mariner*, describes to a large extent the experiences of sailors rounding Cape Horn.

The first chapter of this book is a day-by-day account of the tour of Patagonia conducted by the environmentally conscious company, International Expeditions. Several other tour companies follow essentially the same route. Most of the trip was in Chile. The day spent in Ushuaia is the only excursion into Argentina on the International Expeditions tour.

Chapters 2 through 5 contain in-depth descriptions on various facets of Patagonia. Thus it is hoped that the book will be of interest and help both to readers planning a trip to Patagonia and those who want to learn more about this fascinating part of the world.

CONTENTS

INTRODUCTION ix

I - THE EXPEDITION 1

II - THE ENVIRONMENT 21

III - HISTORY 89

IV - NATIVE GROUPS 127

V - PATAGONIA TODAY 149

APPENDIX 169

BIBLIOGRAPHY 191

INDEX 198

PATAGONIA

*She delivered a river of burning gas and
molten ash, and petrified in the blink of eye mighty
trees, their roots imbedded deep within the volup-
tuous hills of her first born.*

*Fickle Mother Earth! Cataclysmically she trauma-
tized her daughter, the beautiful Patagonia, for the
birthing of her son, the
Andes.*

*Oh, she wept for her daughter Patagonia! The water
leaking from her eyes turned to ice and snow on the
cold cheeks of the Andes.........
the frozen tears of a million years, never to fall on
poor Patagonia.*

*Nervous winds seek solace among rocks, among
scrubs, persistently stirring ancient dust, as they
grieve afresh over the bleached bones of Patagonia.*

*The Atlantic caresses her shore, humming a lullaby,
hush and sleep, hush, hush, hush, as air currents
keep the storm at sea that would quench the thirst of
Patagonia.*

*Restlessly she waits for Father Time to soften the
cold heart of her brother, the Andes. She waits for
the sun to warm his cheek, to melt the tears that
Mother Earth did weep so long ago for her beloved
daughter, the beautiful Patagonia.*

Mary Jo Eisenach

I

THE EXPEDITION

As we got off the plane at Punta Arenas a strong gust of wind blew a broad-brimmed hat off a tour group member's head. I retrieved the hat and wondered if this violent wind is typical of the area. I later learned that indeed it is!

The area around the airport is flat and fairly desolate. The modern bus that took us to the ship stopped first at a restaurant for lunch and then routed us to the Museum Saliesano.

The museum is dark with a dusty odor. The stuffed animals are lumpy but the museum is interesting. Its exhibits show many of the artifacts of the now-extinct Indians as well as early-day life in Patagonia. It displays some models showing the industrial processes of modern-day technology now existing in Punta Arenas.

The *Museo Salesiano de Mayonino (or Maggiorino) Borgatello*, started by an order of Italian missionaries in 1893, is maintained through voluntary contributions. It has an extensive and well-presented collection for a city of this size.

Punta Arenas (Sandy Point) is a city of 130,000 residents and is surprisingly modern. It is the home of a university (University of Magellanes) and is the capitol of the Magellanes Region, one of the thirteen regions of Chile. This region also includes the section of Antarctica claimed by Chile.

For more about the city of Punta Arenas see Chapter 2, page 25.

Boarding our ship, we settled into our cabin and explored our home for the next week. The *MV Terra Australis* (Southern Land) was built in 1983 in Chesapeake Bay by the Chesapeake Shipbuilding Company. For the first years of its existence it cruised on the Mississippi River where it was called the *Savannah*, but it has been in Patagonia since 1991. The ship has a draft of 8 ft (2.44 m) and a maximum speed of ten knots. Its length is 190.5 ft (58.08 m) and its width is 42 ft (12.8 m). It carries a crew of forty when it has a load of 100 or so passengers but it can be operated with a crew of twelve. The ship operates weekly for seven months (from October through April). In its off-season it goes to Valdivia, Chile for maintenance. The *Terra Australis* is owned by a company named *Cruceros Australis* (Southern Cruises). The family of Don Pedo Lecaros of Santiago, Chile owns the company.

The ship is now being equipped with satellite cellphones, specifically for the company's daily communications with the crew. There is radio-telephone communication with the shore used for emergencies and available to any passenger at any time. In emergencies a helicopter can be summoned for winching up a seriously ill or badly injured traveler so that he or she can be quickly transported to a hospital. An alternative method of transportation in an emergency is by means of a Chilean naval vessel. There is a Chilean Naval Base at Puerto Williams as well as navy ships at Punta Arenas. There are also Argentine navy ships based at Ushuaia on Tierra del Fuego Island.

The welcoming ceremony included a review of the safety procedures for the ship, particularly how to put on the life jackets placed in every cabin. During the night the ship left Punta Arenas and proceeded in a southerly direction through the Strait of Magellan.

Marinelli Glacier to Brooks Glacier

In the morning we visited the area opposite the Marinelli Glacier in Ainsworth Bay.

The ship carries four zodiacs (heavy-duty inflatable rubber boats) each carrying some thirteen people, including two or three guides. Each day (usually both morning and afternoon) the zodiacs are lowered into the water, passengers are helped into them, and the boat ferries them to shore. Thus, with two trips of the four boats everyone is transported to whatever site we're observing. Although there is some waiting the system is basically efficient.

In our initial venture in the zodiacs we were awestruck at the sight of glaciers as well as our first experience of wending our way through ice floes. We landed on a low, tundra-like land, which was really a tidal flat. Already there was a pile of five elephant seals yawning at us gawkers. These huge beasts spend some four months of the year on land with the remainder of their year being spent at sea. For more information on elephant seals see Chapter 2, page 65.

Next we walked over the tidal flat to a beaver dam. These industrious creatures have expanded their population from their original base in Argentina into Chile where they have become a nuisance. They dam the rivers to make artificial lakes, and the rising water kills many of the shoreline trees. In addition, of course, many trees are destroyed by the beavers in their ongoing struggle to harvest wood for their dams and lodges. For more about the beavers in Patagonia see Chapter 2, page 59.

Late in the afternoon we sailed into Brooks Bay where we landed close to the Brooks Glacier and some other unnamed glaciers. The guide told us there are some 2000 glaciers in Patagonia, many of them unnamed. Being close to a glacier is an awe-inspiring experience. They are huge, moving ponderously and relentlessly down into the sea. It is evident that they have been melting, undoubtedly due to global warming. Glaciers are discussed in more detail in Chapter 2, page 44.

Glacier and Ice Floes

Photo by Mary Lutz

A blue color is evident within certain places in the crevasses of the glaciers. The reason for the blue color is because glacial ice crystals are so dense that there are few cracks or air bubbles to reflect light. The crystals in the glacier reflect only the short blue wavelengths of light and absorb other visible colors. Thus the ice appears blue. Reportedly the blue is more intense on overcast days.

We gasped as avalanches of snow came hurtling down from glaciers with a boom that sounded like artillery. Also some of the glaciers calved massive chunks of ice thundering off into the sea.

Coming back to the ship we marveled at the show as the ship sailed slowly to the end of Brooks Bay.

Serrano Glacier to the Beagle Channel

The next morning after observing the massive Serrano Glacier from our ship, the tour group members were ferried into Condor Bay. This is a small fjord so named by the crew of the *Terra Australis* because an Andean condor was once seen there. We visited a beach dotted with miniature ice floes that evidently had drifted ashore. An additional excursion was made to the unnamed glacier that is at the end of the narrow fjord. The trip through this magnificent gorge was, for me, the most marvelous experience so far on the trip. The massive monoliths of rock rise almost straight up. Some birds were identified by the professional ornithologists accompanying the group. It was an overwhelming experience. The glacier at the end of the fjord topped the adventure like ice cream on a sumptous cake.

In the late afternoon and early evening the *Terra Australis* sailed into a bay. The water was quiet and the sun shone brightly for several hours. Many different species of birds were sighted. There were not large quantities of birds, only one or two of each species. With the massive rock formations looming above us this was a delightful experience.

In this cul-de-sac bay we saw the first boat we had seen since leaving Punta Arenas. It was located in a tiny inlet and almost hidden from view. As we sailed slowly into the larger cove, the top of the mast and supporting shrouds came into view. We speculated that it might be a weather station or antenna.

Then we saw, to our surprise, that it was a sailboat, perhaps 25 or 30 ft (8 or 9 m) in length. We spotted someone on board. Since we had seen virtually no signs of civilization since Punta Arenas this was exciting! Then started the speculation as to what they were doing there. Guesses ran from a couple on a honeymoon, to a recluse, or a smuggler. This last speculation collapsed when it was pointed out that there was nothing to smuggle down here at the bottom of the world!

Our ship blew its horn and a shrill answering blast came from the little yacht.

We never found out what it was doing in this locale—certainly one of the most remote in the world.

In the evening, after dinner, a full rainbow appeared, shining all the way from horizon to horizon.

Avenue of Glaciers to Yendegaia Ranch to Puerto Williams

Rising early we viewed the series of glaciers on the north side of the Beagle Channel.

This area is called the Avenue of the Glaciers because they appear in a row one after the other. Some of the glaciers do not extend down into the water as do those we had seen until now. Waterfalls sometimes descend into the water from the glaciers which end a few dozen yards above the Beagle Channel.

The ship turned into Yendegaia Bay (*yende* means deep in the Yaghan language and the ending *aia* means bay). Anchoring a few hundred yards off shore, we zodiaced in to the ranch. The headquarters consists of four low hut-like buildings. The ranch is privately owned by a group from Punta Arenas. There are horses available for rent, but we chose to hike into this beautiful area. Although not a steep climb the trail wound up, down, and around for a mile or two. The ranch is hilly and intermittently covered with low vegetation. There were many small flowers. We stopped at an overlook to see the Five Pyramids, a series of five mountain peaks. Condor Mountain is off to the left. The view from this point is breathtaking, looking out over the varied terrain. Part of the scene includes the shallow part of Yendegaia Bay in front of the beautiful mountains.

We saw Andean condors circling high in the sky (see Chapter 2, page 72) and guanaco feeding on the sides of the mountains above the timberline (see Chapter 2, page 50). Upon returning we looked into one of the ranch buildings where a few of the ranch workmen live. Needless to say, they have rather spartan quarters.

Reboarding our ship we continued on eastward in the Beagle Channel. Here the Beagle Channel constitutes the boundary between Chile and Argentina. We passed Ushuaia on our left and proceeded on to Puerto Williams. We had a pleasant stop in this little community, walking to view a beaver dam, then visiting the museum. In the company of the ship's doctor and his wife, my wife Mary and I then walked through the town. Due to a sudden rainstorm, we sought shelter in the Naval Chapel, which includes a beautiful wooden carving.

For detailed information about Puerto Williams, see Chapter 2, page 31.

Ushuaia to Tierra del Fuego National Park

We docked at Ushuaia, Argentina late at night and when we looked out of the cabin window in the morning we saw not only the city of Ushuaia but a Russian ship that was moored at the pier. By the way, border formalities were already taken care of by the crew, as they had collected our passports at the beginning of the trip.

The city of Ushuaia (population 35,000) was founded by the missionary Thomas Bridges in 1869. A prison was, for decades, the primary reason for the existence of the city. Started in 1896, the prison was initially for second-offenders, both men and women plus a few children. But it subsequently housed dangerous criminals and political prisoners.

Ushuaia is the southernmost city on the planet. Because it has a deepwater port it now thrives on tourism, as well as activities related to forest exploitation such as furniture manufacturing. It also has a small fishing industry. Sheep raising and beaver-trapping are two other local activities.

Something of a boom town, Ushuaia has relatively high wages for its residents. Along with the tax advantages of living in Tierra del Fuego many Argentines come here in search of wealth.

The city overlooks the harbor, and many of its houses are concrete. A few are partially metal and some of these are historic homes that have been restored. Also, there are a few sledge homes. These are homes from long ago which were built on sleds, so that they could be moved if the land under the house was sold. There are several ski areas nearby, including at least one that operates year-round.

Until recent decades the city of Ushuaia was quite isolated. For example, in 1930 no ship reached the town for ten months. Even in better years a letter could take forty-five days or more to reach its destination, and newspapers took months. Then, in 1943, the Maritime Government of Tierra del Fuego was established.

Soon thereafter the prison was closed and the modern development of Ushuaia really began.

In 1968 Patagonia was declared a priority area of Argentina and the national government began channeling money to the area as never before. The government had declared the area a tax-free zone and, in subsequent years, promoted economic development through the establishment of tax exemptions for industry. The downtown area is lined with duty-free shops selling a variety of local products. The International Expeditions tour allows several hours in Ushuaia. A small museum facing the Beagle Channel, the *Museo del Fin del Mundo* (Museum at the End of the World), is worth visiting. Also, the former prison on the east side of town is quite interesting. More information about the history of Ushuaia is located in Chapter 2, page 28.

Next we went to Tierra del Fuego National Park, we saw the mountains of the Darwin Range from the Argentinian side of the Andes. We again viewed signs of beaver encroachment and heard more about the devastation caused by them. We also walked part of the way on a spongy muck of peat moss that felt like walking on jello.

The guide on this walk was Argentine, since apparently our Chilean guides are not allowed to do their thing in Argentina.

Taken to one end of the "railroad at the end of the world" we boarded for the short ride on this train. Although it is not a commercial railroad at this time, the narrow gauge line remains as a vestige of the old line used by the convicts of the Ushuaia Prison from 1902 to 1947. The prisoners would take this train to cut down trees in what is now the Tierra del Fuego National Park.

I had assumed that Paul Theroux's book, *The Old Patagonian Express,* was about this line but I was mistaken. The book's title refers to a railroad much farther north in the Argentine part of Patagonia.

After the train ride we bussed to a restaurant on the outskirts of Ushuaia where we had a lamb barbecue lunch and then shopped in this pleasant, bustling city. The most memorable picture for me was the blossoming display of huge multicolored lupines in the restaurant's garden. That evening, before the sumptuous dinner, we were treated to a delightful demonstration of Argentine folk dancing.

Garibaldi Glacier

Backtracking into the Beagle Channel, we again passed through the Avenue of the Glaciers in the early morning. Gliding into the Pia Fjord the reflection in the surprisingly still water was magnificent. The glaciers and mountains were almost perfectly mirrored on the water's surface. After anchoring the ship, we took the small boats into a rocky outcropping only a few hundred yards off the Pia Glacier. Maintaining a minute or so of silence, our group heard rumbling from inside the glacier. From time to time, a small piece of ice would calve off the glacier and fall into the water. While we stood there, marveling at both the sights and the sounds, the sun came out from behind the clouds. It was a never-to-be-forgotten moment.

It had been a somewhat cloudy day up to this time. As the sun shone brightly on the reflections in the water it momentarily appeared as if there were a sheet of ice under the water. This marvelous fantasy existed for only a few seconds before the effect disappeared.

Before boarding the zodiac we were served "glacier ice drinks." The guides go down to the water, bring back a chunk of age-old ice, break it up and serve it in whiskey or hot chocolate drinks. Kind of corny, but fun.

As each boat lands, the crew sets up a gangplank with a railing on one side. Then they help the passengers get on and off the boat. It is surprising how many of the passengers use canes and walking sticks.

On both the way to and returning from the Pia Glacier we passed close to a tiny rocky island that was covered with noisy kelp gulls. The island is evidently a nesting area and the few skirmishes going on between the gulls amused us all.

In the afternoon we didn't leave the ship but the *Terra Australis* cruised slowly into the narrow channel that is Garibaldi Sound. We came close to two family groups of noisy sea lions on

the rocks with a handful of turkey vultures above
the rocky shore. The noisy antics of the seagoing
mammals provided plenty of entertainment.
Also, we had a clear view of an Andean condor
that left its rocky perch and soared over us. Late
in the day we even spotted whales. To learn more
about these and other animals, see Chapter 2,
page 50.

During the night the ship pushed westward
through the Beagle Channel, then turned north
for a short distance through the open ocean. Turning back east it proceeded among the Patagonian
Islands.

Tucker Island to Porvenir

This morning we sailed eastward through
Gabriel Channel past an ice sheet that is atop the
mountains. The sheet is said to be 15 km (more
than 9 mi) long. We then got into the zodiacs for
a ride around Tucker Island. This is a bird paradise so we refrained from landing in order not to
disturb them. There were hundreds of cormorants, both rocks and kings. Also a few kelp geese,
but the stars of today's outing were the dozens
of penguins. It was a surprise to see these Magellanic penguins up on the rocks, perhaps 50 ft
(15 m) up to the highest point on the tiny island.
Yesterday we had seen a sea lion on the rocks
perhaps 20 ft (6 m) up. It is amazing how these,
seemingly awkward sea animals can maneuver
on land.

Late in the afternoon we anchored in the bay leading to the town of Porvenir. This town is the capitol of the Chilean part of Tierra del Fuego as well as its largest town. More details about the town can be found in Chapter 2, page 30.

We took the small boats to shore where we were met by buses and vans that took our group through the town of Porvenir and also to an *estancia* (ranch). The drive through the countryside was different from what we had seen until now. There were no glaciers or mountains in evidence. Only treeless rolling hills that showed little signs of civilization. The desolate landscape was mostly covered with a low shrub reminiscent of mesquite (but greener). There were several ponds along the way and we saw guanaco, black-necked swans, and other unusual birds. Sometimes flamingos are seen in these ponds. See Chapter Two, page 83 for more about flamingos.

There seem to be a number of unoccupied buildings in Porvenir; apparently there is not much to attract people here. There is a Croatian population in town and on the ranches (mostly sheep, some cattle). Many European immigrants have settled in Patagonia and the ethnic groups tend to stay together.

Magdalena Island to Punta Arenas

Today we had what in my opinion was the peak experience of the whole trip. Early in the morning we went to Magdalena Island to walk among the penguins. This island, a Chilean national monument, is literally covered with Magellanic penguins. Estimates of the population there vary from 100,000 to 250,000. A professional ornithologist in our group estimated 200,000. That's good enough for me.

The penguins come to this refuge in October and stay until March for the purpose of breeding and raising their young. Families cluster around burrows (some of the birds actually hunker down inside them). Although people are restricted to an area near the beach, the penguins ignore the roped-off area. They waddle down to the ocean, paying little attention to the gawkers taking their pictures. Sometimes they even get curious and walk up to people to nip at their clothing.

This type of penguin is also called the Jackass penguin because of the braying sound it makes. Being among these tens of thousands of the cute little creatures is an overwhelming experience. The humility one feels in the middle of this natural environment is almost inexpressible.

Later, the ship docked in Punta Arenas and, after saying goodby to our tour group friends who were not going on the extension of the tour to Torres del Paine, we were bussed into town where we drove around briefly and were shown some of the historic buildings and other sights. After lunch in Punta Arenas, we took off in a very comfortable bus to Torres del Paine.

The first several miles of the six-hour trip we went straight across the pampas. The land was treeless, flat, and dry but surprisingly green. Later the land grew more varied with trees and rolling hills. We saw guanacos, Lesser rheas, and many other unusual birds. It was a scenic drive. Arriving at our destination, a hotel on a working ranch, called the *Mirador el Payne*, we had an excellent beef dinner.

Torres del Paine National Park

This day, again, was an exceptional one. It began with a long bus trip around and into the Torres del Paine Park. Although somewhat an overcast day we saw most of the fantastic mountain range. Before stopping for lunch our group walked into an area where we overlooked *Salto Grande* (big waterfall). It was an extremely windy walk—we were almost blown away. The williwaw (the famed Patagonian wind) was the strongest wind I have ever experienced.

After a short ride in the bus we walked on a footbridge to lunch at a hotel on an island in a serene lake. After driving awhile and seeing some more astounding vistas we next visited another spectacular locale. Walking a few hundred yards into this forested area, we came across several Austral parakeets (see Chapter 2, page 84).

Next, we crossed a suspension bridge over the raging Pinto River. Only two people at a time are allowed on the bridge. Not only that, but during today's trip there were several times when everyone had to get out of the bus and walk across the bridge, while the bus came across without its passengers. The Chileans seem concerned about the weight-bearing capacity of their bridges!

A few hundred yards down the path past the parakeets we came to an open area facing a body of water filled with huge ice floes in fantastic shapes. These floes have come off the Grey Glacier and have been blown across Lake Grey to this point. The whole scene was eerie and calm.

After our return to the bus we began the lengthy ride back to our hotel. It took so long not only because there was a distance to cover but also because we stopped so often to view and photograph the fascinating array of wildlife we saw on this remarkable excursion.

We saw dozens of guanacos in groups varying in size from one to eight. There were many baby guanacos (called *chulengos*) one of whom was nursing. We were told the chulengos were about two months old. The guanaco is a fascinating animal. The animals are easy to photograph in this park.

Condors were a frequent sight. At one place we stopped to photograph a group of some thirteen of them, apparently attracted by a dead animal. The Andean condor is the largest land bird in the world capable of flight.

We saw a few Lesser rheas, an ostrich-like bird, and one had six little ones along. The guide said they were probably only about two weeks old and since they were born late in the birthing season they might not survive the coming winter. Detailed facts about the rhea can be found in Chapter 2, page 77.

It was now early February, so the weather would turn bitter cold by April. When thinking about the weather in Patagonia it is easiest to think in terms of it being six months different from the Northern Hemisphere. In other words, April is equivalent to October, May to November, and so on. Actually, winter comes a little earlier in Patagonia than it does in most of the Northern Hemisphere even allowing for the half year difference.

On today's outing we also saw a few southern grey foxes and many unusual birds such as the caracara (striated, crested, and white-throated), the coscoroba swan, the black-necked swan, and others. More information about all the unusual wildlife can be found in Chapter 2, beginning with page 50.

Torres del Paine National Park to Milodon Cave to Puerto Natales

In the morning we rested and walked a bit around this working farm. After a lamb barbecue for lunch we drove to the Milodon Cave. This

cave is a well-appointed national monument. It
has a small museum containing some information about the cave and the discovery of the remains of an ancient giant sloth. To read more
about the cave see Chapter 2, page 43.

We then drove the few miles to Puerto
Natales where we checked in to the four-star
Hotel CostAustralis.

Punta Arenas to Santiago

After breakfast we boarded the bus for Punta
Arenas, and stopped for lunch (another delicious
lamb barbecue) at the *Hosterîa Rîo Verde*, which
Americans would call an inn. A fascinating mu-
seum-like atmosphere made us wish we could
stay and spend time with the very hospitable
family who owned and ran this combination
hotel and working farm. Before we moved on
we watched a short demonstration of dogs herd-
ing sheep.

Sadly, the tour was now complete and we
flew home with a desire to learn more about this
fabulous place—*Patagonia, At the Bottom of the
World.*

II

THE ENVIRONMENT

THE LAND

The history of the unique terrain of Patagonia goes way back. Scientists think that throughout the entire Pleistocene period (1.8 million to 11,000 years ago) the western part of Patagonia was periodically buried beneath huge ice fields. The largest expansion of the ice fields occurred around one million years ago although the advance and withdrawal of the glaciers continued. It is believed that the last major advance occurred between 30,000 and 15,000 years ago. Even today you will see the effects of the receding glaciers accelerated by the global warming that is man's contribution to the processes of nature. As the ice fields began melting the water ran off into the oceans. The draining of powerful ice-streams to the east created the large lakes of present-day

Argentina, while the draining to the west and south created the deep fjords that have split up so much of the western area into a mosaic of islands.

On your trip you will probably hear mention of "moraines." These are mounds of dirt, gravel, rocks, or other material at the former limits of glaciers. Terminal moraines are those at the farthest extent of a glacier while lateral moraines are those on the side of a moving body of snow and ice.

There are two narrow stretches of the Strait of Magellan called *Primera Angostura* and *Segunda Angostura*. Glaciologists think that these channels were cut by the meltwater from glaciers over a period of thousands of years ending about 9,000 years ago.

Tierra del Fuego

> *To the south we had a scene of savage magnificence, well becoming Tierra del Fuego. There was a degree of mysterious grandeur in mountain behind mountain, with the deep intervening valleys, all covered by one thick, dusky mass of forest. The atmosphere, likewise, in this climate, where gale succeeds gale, with rain, hail, and sleet, seems blacker than anywhere else. In the Strait of Magellan, looking due*

southward from Port Famine, the distant channels between the mountains appeared from their gloominess to lead beyond the confines of this world.

Charles Darwin, *The Voyage of the Beagle*, 1845

This huge island (Isla Grande de Tierra del Fuego) is about the size of Vermont and New Hampshire combined. From north to south it extends from the Strait of Magellan to the Beagle Channel, and from east to west it spans from the Atlantic to the Pacific. The Strait of Magellan separates it from the mainland of South America. Shaped somewhat like a triangle with the Beagle Channel as its base, the Atlantic Ocean on one side and the Strait of Magellan on the other, it extends all the way to the Pacific Ocean near its base.

Tierra del Fuego includes mountains as high as Monte Sarmiento, 7,550 ft (2,300 m) and Monte Darwin, 7,999 ft (2,438 m), and mountain glaciers. These mountains are the southern tip of the Andes Mountains.

Split between Argentina and Chile by a north-south border which runs through the island, Tierra del Fuego is roughly two-thirds Chile and one-third Argentina.

The terrain of the island varies a great deal. Most of the northern portion is under 600 ft (180 m) in height, and the Atlantic coastal area is low-lying. This area contains many lakes and moraines. The southern and western parts are the mountainous areas, with vegetation limited to mosses and stunted trees. The central part of the island is heavily forested but the northern prairies are covered with the tussock grass and referred to as *las pampas*.

After Magellan's voyage, three hundred fifty years went by before colonization by Chilean and Argentine nationals began. This was sparked by the introduction of sheep farming, the discovery of gold, and the hunting of seals and whales.

In 1945, oil was discovered at Manantiales in the northern part of Tierra del Fuego thus creating Chile's only oil field. There are now pipelines to the Strait of Magellan, while a small refinery meets local needs.

Some timber harvesting takes place in the forested areas of the island. Other industries include fish and crayfish canning at Ushuaia, Argentina, and Porvenir, Chile. Also hunting for nutria and seal and the trapping of beaver takes place. Cattle farming is a significant industry, while sheep farming is a declining enterprise with most surplus sheep processing on the mainland. However, there is a small meat refrigeration plant located at Río Grande in Argentina.

There are no railways in Tierra del Fuego and roads are poor. However, there are airports at Ushuaia and Río Gallegos. Transportation is mainly by sea, with regular service between

Porvenir and Punta Arenas. Both the Argentine and Chilean navies are active in the area, particularly in the Beagle Channel, supplying Ushuaia and Puerto Williams.

The Argentine part of Tierra del Fuego is 8,329 sq mi (21,571 sq km) The capital of this part of Tierra del Fuego is Ushuaia, the southernmost city in the world, located on the Beagle Channel. Textile and electronic firms are in operation at Río Grande and Ushuaia, the island's two main cities. Fishing includes spider crabs, mussels, and other mollusks, which are canned and exported. Krill, tiny shrimplike creatures that are the main food of most whales and other sea animals, are extremely abundant in adjoining ocean waters. They could serve in the future as a source of food for humans.

Punta Arenas

Because Punta Arenas is located on one of the world's historic trade routes, its prosperity has risen and fallen with that trade. Its very isolation from the rest of Chile, in effect, contributed to its progress. This was because, in the latter half of the nineteenth century, many of its citizens had been forced into exile or, for whatever reason, chose to leave the main part of Chile.

Originally a convict settlement, Punta Arenas is still the only city on the Strait of Magellan. According to Lucas Bridges, son of missionary

Thomas Bridges (see Chapter 3, page 118), it had
a convict population of 600 in 1842. Punta Arenas was officially founded in 1848 to maintain
Chile's claim to the strait. But it suffered from
the practice of banishing difficult soldiers to this
remote region.

In 1851 a violent and erratic Lieutenant
named Cambiazo overthrew the local governor,
who was later killed, and Cambiazo began a
reign of terror reminiscent of the time before the
French Revolution. For three months there was
panic, anarchy, and destruction in Punta Arenas.
Cambiazo apparently had no plan for gover-
nance, but simply acted on his whims. Among
other schemes, he deceived and took over some
foreign ships that were anchored in the bay. Finally captured, Cambiazo was executed along
with several of his followers. The city was then
looted by Tehuelche Indians. Then, in 1877, a
third uprising took place in which again there
was much bloodshed. This one was the result of
a rampage by soldiers, prisoners, and prostitutes!

Surviving this third blow, the city eventually
prospered, and by 1881 was a bustling port of
nearly 2,000—with a church, a small fort, several dozen houses, and, of course, the prison.
Later in that decade Punta Arenas was the site of
a meeting between the presidents of Argentina
and Chile in which war between the two countries was averted.

During the California Gold Rush Punta Arenas became a haven for clipper ships sailing from the East Coast of the United States to San Francisco. The advent of the steam ship actually increased the marine traffic in Punta Arenas, because it had now become much less perilous to navigate the Strait of Magellan. Ships were thus able to avoid the terrible Cape Horn route.

The first wave of immigrants from Europe came in the 1880s. Settlers arrived from Spain, Portugal, Russia, Switzerland, Yugoslavia, and England. By 1890, half the people were foreigners. Huge fortunes were accumulated by several of these immigrants, largely from sheep and cattle ranching.

Before the building of the Panama Canal, Punta Arenas was a busy coaling station and has now become an important center for the export of Patagonian wool and mutton. Oil is also exported from the nearby oil fields. Sawmills, machine repair shops, forestry-related industries, and fishing are also important to the economy. In recent years, tourism has become a significant industry.

In addition to the *Museo Salesiano* described in Chapter I there are two other museums.

The Braun-Menendez Regional Museum, officially the Historical Museum of Magallanes, is located within the Braun-Menéndez Mansion, a national monument. Inaugurated in February,

1983, the museum traces the discovery, colonization, and development of the Magallanes region through historical objects, illustrations, and photographs. It also includes a library and an art collection.

The Patagonian Institute is primarily a research center. It is located in a cluster of small houses on the grounds of the local university. It displays various scientific and technological artifacts. There is a library, a botanical garden, a handicraft store, and the *Museo del Recuerdo* (Old Time Museum), with its collection of restored carriages, machines, and tools used in pioneering times. There is also a maritime exhibit, and an example of a typical house from colonial times.

Ushuaia

Ushuaia (the word means inner port on the west in the Yaghan language) is today a bustling port of some 35,000 people. It is the capital of the Argentine province (*provincia*) of Tierra del Fuego. Ushuaia (pronounced *oosh-WY-ya*) is the southernmost city in the world. An Argentine naval base was established here in 1884, and in 1893, after Tierra del Fuego was partitioned between Argentina and Chile, Ushuaia was officially designated a city. Development in Ushuaia continued at a slow pace and it was actually not until 1956 that the first automobile appeared.

From 1897 on, the prisoners logged trees out in the forest to supply a sawmill. The prisoners were transported into the forest on a railroad that was built for that purpose.

A prisoner of the time wrote a letter describing the conditions of some of the prisoners: "Convicts who could not bear the cruel harassment have hung themselves; others died of anemia or TB. Bear in mind that those prisoners sentenced to 'permanent confinement' were not allowed to read, to receive letters, to smoke, not even to drink maté and were given only half their ration."

Other prisoners, though, were apparently more fortunate and were paid for their logging work. Upon their release from prison many of the men married women in the community and remained in Ushuaia. At its peak the prison contained over 1,000 convicts. At one time, an estimated ninety percent of the town's citizens worked at the prison or provided services to it.

The convicts contributed a great deal to the development of the town. For instance, they were responsible for the introduction of electricity to the city in 1901 and they were the first firemen. Their labor built the pier and the post office as well as many other construction projects. Some of the wood they cut heated the city or helped in the city's early development.

From 1896 to 1947 some of Argentina's most notorious prisoners were housed here. In 1902 a wooden "railway" was established with oxen hauling wagons along wooden rails. By 1908 this had been replaced by a regular railroad which was used to take the prisoners into the forest for their timber cutting. Today that railroad has been turned into a tourist attraction and is now in the Tierra del Fuego National Park. Among the other scenic vistas on the rail line are the dead stumps remaining still from the trees logged by the prisoners.

In 1988 a scientific research station was established near Ushuaia for the purpose of measuring the ozone depletion in the atmosphere. One of six such sites around the world, the station is funded by the U.S. National Science Foundation. It operates with the cooperation of the Argentine government.

Porvenir

This is the capital of the Chilean section of Tierra del Fuego. A sleepy town, it has a population of 6,386 inhabitants, but still offers all the urban services such as hotels, restaurants, banks, and communication systems. Many of its citizens are descendants of Croatian immigrants, who arrived in the 19th century in search of gold.

Porvenir was formerly the center of marine and commercial activities in Tierra del Fuego, but today Ushuaia instead plays that role. Porvenir's main economic resources today are oil, livestock, and king crab. A small amount of gold is still extracted.

Puerto Williams

This little community on Navarino Island (*Isla Navarino*) bills itself as "the southernmost year-around community in the world." It has about 2,500 residents, many of whom are descendants of the Indians who used to live in the area. Its purpose for being is the Chilean Naval Base there, founded in 1953. However, it has some retail businesses and there are even two cybercafes, proving that the Internet is truly worldwide.

Its most interesting feature is the *Museo Martin Gusinde*, named after the German Catholic priest who worked among the Yaghan Indians in this region. Although small, the museum is interesting in that it pictures both the life of the priest and of the Yaghans. There are also a few bedraggled stuffed specimens of wildlife from the area. Another pleasant place to visit is the Naval Chapel with its Sea Madonna statue. The wood in the church is exceptionally beautiful.

In size, *Isla Navarino* is about 60 mi (100 km) in an east-west direction and approximately 25 mi (40 km) from north to south. The island is dominated by a mountain range called *Cordon de los Dientes*, an extremely craggy range that stretches in an east-west direction through the northern part of the island. Interestingly enough, there are many guanaco on this island, and since there are no predators (e.g. pumas) they are less shy than in many other parts of Patagonia.

Cape Horn

This rocky island is about 60 mi (100 km) south of Puerto Williams. It is in the most fearsome (and feared) stretch of ocean in the world, Drake Strait (also known as Drake Passage.) At latitude 55° 59′ S and longitude 67° 12′ WS, the famous Horn is some 1,300 miles farther south than Africa's Cape of Good Hope and 600 miles below the latitude of New Zealand's Stewart Island. It is the farthest crag of earth pointing toward the icy continent of Antarctica. It is truly at the very bottom of the world.

Before 1520 it was believed that the world was divided by the landmass that we now call North and South America. From then until the opening of the Panama Canal, "doubling the Horn" (or sailing through the Strait of Magellan) was the only way by sea from the east coast of North America.

Since the opening of the Panama Canal in 1914 the Cape has seen little traffic. Yet today, with the building of bigger and bigger ships, some so big they can't get through the tried-and-true Central American ditch, it seems possible that "rounding the horn" may again become a common route for mariners. During the Golden Age of Sail, from the sixteenth to the twentieth centuries, Cape Horn was the most imposing obstacle on the world's oceans. *It still is!*

Sailing ships usually had a rough time while getting from the Atlantic to the Pacific via Drake

Strait, the water south of Cape Horn. The reason that the Drake Strait has the most violent seas in the world is because the winds, primarily from the west, are deflected by the Andes Mountains. The Andes constitute the longest mountain range on earth and one of the highest. Wind always seeks the easiest path, so it's easier to go around the mountains than over them. Another factor is that in this way the Andes also spawn vicious little cyclones that cause the winds to be anything but predictable. In addition the prevailing currents around the southern hemisphere go in a westerly direction. Tides actually enter the Drake Strait from both directions, adding to the confusion. The combination of wind, current, and tide makes for a violently tempestuous strait.

RichardHenry Dana, in *Two Years Before the Mast*, describes the ordeal this way:

> *'Here comes Cape Horn!' said the chief mate; and we hardly had time to haul done and clew up before it was upon us. In a few minutes a heavier sea was raised than I had ever seen, and as it was directly ahead, the little brig, which was no better than a bathing-machine, plunged into it, and all the forward part of her was under water; the sea pouring in through the bow-ports and hawse-holes and over the*

knight-heads, threatening to wash everything overboard. In the lee scuppers it was up to a man's waist. We sprang aloft and double-reefed the topsails, and furled the other sails, and made all snug. But this would not do; the brig was laboring and straining against the head sea, and the gale was growing worse and worse. At the same time sleet and hail were driving with all fury against us. We clewed down, and hauled out the reef-tackles again, and close-reefed the foretopsail, and furled the main, and hove her to, on the starboard tack. Here was an end to our fine prospects. We made up our minds to head winds and cold weather; sent down the royal yards, and unrove the gear; but all the rest of the top hamper remained aloft, even to the sky-sail masts and studding-sail booms.

Throughout the night it stormed violently,—rain, hail, snow, and sleet beating upon the vessel,—the wind continued ahead, and the sea running high. At daybreak (about 3 a.m.) the deck was covered with snow...The clouds cleared away at sunrise, and, the wind becoming more fair, we again made sail and stood nearly up to our course.

And two days later:
Towards morning the wind went down, and during the whole forenoon we lay tossing about in a dead calm, and in the midst of a thick fog. The calms here are unlike those in most parts of the world, for here there is generally so high a sea running, with periods of calm so short that it has no time to go down; and vessels, being under no command of sails or rudder, lie like logs upon the water. We were obliged to steady the booms and yards by guys and braces, and to lash everything well below.

And two days later still:
A true specimen of Cape Horn was coming upon us. A great cloud of a dark slate-color was driving on us from the southwest; and we did our best to take in sail (for the light sails had been set during the first part of the day) before we were in the midst of it. We had got the light sails furled, the courses hauled up, and the topsail reef-tackles hauled out, and were just mounting the fore-rigging when the storm struck us. In an instant the sea, which had been comparatively quiet, was running higher and higher; and it became almost as dark as night. The

> *hail and sleet were harder than I had yet felt them; seeming almost to pin us down to the rigging. We were longer taking in sail than ever before; for the sails were stiff and wet, the ropes and rigging covered with snow and sleet, and we ourselves cold and nearly blinded with the violence of the storm. By the time we had got down upon deck again, the little brig was plunging madly into a tremendous head sea, which at every drive rushed in through the bow-ports and over the bows, and buried all the forward part of the vessel.*

The above was written while rounding the horn from the Atlantic to the Pacific but when Dana's ship returned around the horn (from the Pacific to the Atlantic) they ran into an even more severe storm and it took them eight days to round Cape Horn. This was in 1834—36 and the voyage was from Boston to California and back.

From the *Voyage Of the Beagle* by Charles Darwin:

> *On the 11th of January, 1833, by carrying a press of sail, we fetched within a few miles of the great rugged mountain of York Minster ... when a violent squall compelled us to shorten sail*

and stand out to sea. The surf was breaking fearfully on the coast, and the spray was carried over a cliff estimated to 200 feet in height. On the 12th the gale was very heavy, and we did not know exactly where we were: it was a most unpleasant sound to hear constantly repeated, "keep a good look-out to leeward." On the 13th the storm raged with its full fury: our horizon was narrowly limited by the sheets of spray borne by the wind. The sea looked ominous, like a dreary waving plain with patches of drifted snow: whilst the ship laboured heavily, the albatross glided with its expanded wings right up the wind. At noon a great sea broke over us, and filled one of the whale boats, which was obliged to be instantly cut away. The poor Beagle trembled at the shock, and for a few minutes would not obey her helm; but soon, like a good ship that she was, she righted and came up to the wind again. Had another sea followed the first, our fate would have been decided soon, and for ever. We had now been twenty-four days trying in vain to get westward; the men were worn out with fatigue, and they had not had for many nights or days a dry thing to put on.

*Captain Fitz Roy gave up the attempt
to get westward by the outside coast.*

From *The Captive In Patagonia* (1853), by
BenjaminFranklin Bourne: "The most dif ficult
and dangerous feature of navigation in the straits
is the encountering of sudden and violent squalls,
which strike the vessel without the least warning, and are frequently enough to wreck her in a
few minutes, even in the hands of most experienced seamen."

Other intrepid sailors spent days, even weeks,
fighting the contrary winds while rounding the
horn. And some, like the notorious Captain Bligh,
simply gave up and turned around. An excerpt
from Bligh's journal:

> *The stormy weather continued with a
> great sea. The ship now began to com-
> plain, and required to be pumped ev-
> ery hour; which was no more than we
> had reason to expect from such a con-
> tinuance of gales of wind and high
> seas...Every morning all the ham-
> mocks were taken down from where
> they hung, and, when the weather was
> too bad to keep them upon deck, they
> were put in the cabin; so that the be-
> tween decks were cleaned daily, and
> aired with fires, if the hatches could not
> be opened. With all this bad weather,*

> *we had the additional mortification to find, at the end of every day, that we were losing ground; for notwithstanding our utmost exertions, and keeping on the most advantageous tacks, (which, if the weather had been at all moderate, would have sufficiently answered our purpose) yet the greater part of the time, we were doing little better than drifting with the wind.*

Of course, with the coming of powered ships, the traverse became less dangerous, although no less harrowing.

In 1962, the Chilean government placed a 13 ft (4 m) high light tower some 130 ft (40 m) up on the rock island that is Cape Horn. This seems to be like shutting the barn door after the horse is stolen, as there is very little traffic around the Horn today.

Rest assured if you take the *Terra Australis*—it does not go around Cape Horn!

Strait of Magellan

The Strait of Magellan is the body of water that separates the mainland of South America from the island of Tierra del Fuego. Magellan sailed through this passage in thirty-eight days. He thought it was tough sailing but he really had it relatively easy. Of the next twenty-one ships to attempt sailing through this new passage to the Orient, twelve sank.

Varying in width from less than 2 mi (3 km), to 20 mi (32 km), at Punta Arenas, the Strait is like a river winding snake-like from the Atlantic to the Pacific. Stretching some 368 mi (592 km) it is affected by the tides in both oceans as well as by the willilaws coming off the Andes. The currents, too, make it difficult to navigate and it seems almost unbelievable that a wind-powered ship could actually maneuver safely through this serpentine channel.

Beagle Channel

The Beagle Channel was named for the British ship *Beagle*, in which Charles Darwin explored the area (1833–34). This strait is the southern boundary of the island of Tierra del Fuego. The channel runs in an east-west direction and is about 150 mi (240 km) long and 3 to 8 mi (5 to 13 km) wide. It separates Tierra del Fuego from Navarino, Hoste, and other smaller islands to the south. Towards the west the channel splits into two branches that go around *Isla Gordon.*

The eastern part of the channel is the Chile–Argentina border, while the western portion is entirely within Chile. At the channel's eastern end, the islands of Picton, Nueva, and Lennox were the subject of a border dispute between Chile and Argentina that began in the 1840s and which almost led to war between the two nations in 1978. The Beagle Channel had been under the control of Chile but the military government of Argentina threatened Chile with war unless they gave up control of the Channel. The Chilean military government, under General Pinochet, refused, the Vatican intervened, and Argentina capitulated.

Only a few years later in 1982 Chile and Argentina were close to war. An international arbitration finally recognized as Chilean the Beagle Channel islands–Picton, Nueva, and Lennox. Argentina eventually backed down.

The dispute did not officially end until May 2, 1985, when a treaty awarding the three islands to Chile went into effect.

The treaty delineated some 60 mi (100 km) of border between the two countries. It gave Chile control over the Strait of Magellan, divided the huge island of Tierra del Fuego, and gave all lands south of Tierra del Fuego to Chile.

The agreement introduces a new era in which the border serves as a "unifying bridge" instead of a "separating wall." Evidence of that improved relationship include joint military maneuvers, Chilean investment in the Argentine economy, and plans for gas and oil pipelines between the two.

Torres del Paine (or Payne)

This Chilean national park is a UNESCO Biosphere Reserve. The Torres in the name translates as 'towers' while the Paine (pronounced 'pienee') either means 'blue' in one of the Indian languages or is the name of an early explorer. Take your pick.

Torres del Paine is a huge park of 598,604 acres (242,242 hectares). It is almost the size of Yosemite National Park in the United States. The scenery is simply stunning. The feature that gives the park its name is also its most famous: three granite peaks rise almost straight up from the surrounding terrain. These huge phallic symbols reach over 9,000 ft (2,800 m) and are some of the most photogenic mountains in the world. And yes (to answer your question), they have been climbed.

Somewhat lower, and of a different geological make-up are the three mountains known as the *Cuernos del Paine* (Horns of Paine.) These display the intrusion of granite rock (white) into sedimentary rock (black). The result is a sort of black roof over white siding, which makes for a spectacular and unique vista. From one angle one can view the *Cuernos del Paine* in front of the Torres del Paine. Breathtaking!

There are many other mountains in the park along with lakes, waterfalls, glaciers, desert areas, and forests. Some of the lakes are a brilliant blue in certain weather conditions and others are green. Accommodations are surprisingly comfortable. Of particular delight is lunch at a restaurant on an island in one of the beautiful lakes. Unfortunately, sometimes rain clouds partially (or even totally) block the views of the mountains.

Milodon Cave

Near Puerto Natales is the famous Milodon Cave—famous, not only because of the remains of the giant sloth that were found there, but also because of the excitement that followed its discovery.

Some years after the sloth's appearance in 1895 a London newspaper dispatched a reporter to Patagonia because of the rumor that a giant sloth still existed in the area. Of course, there was no sloth. What was found were some exceptionally well-preserved pieces of sloth skin as well as a considerable amount of dung. The giant ground sloth was some 9 ft (3 m) tall. Also found in the cave were relics that proved the existence of five other extinct animals. They were a horse, a large mammal about the size of a horse, two different camelids (relatives of the still-existing guanaco), and a large cat. Radiocarbon dating of these remains indicated that the sloth lived between 13,000 and 10,000 years ago. Thus they may well have co-existed with humans.

The cave itself is 100 ft (30 m) high, 260 ft (80 m) wide, and 660 ft (200 m) deep. It is not of interest because of its size but rather because of what was found there. In addition to a path back into the cave there is an impressive life-size model of what the ground sloth must have looked like.

Glaciers

Glaciers are fascinating phenomena of nature. Ten percent of the land area of the earth is covered with glaciers. Glaciers and the ice fields that spawn them contain about seventy percent of the world's freshwater, and if they all should melt some day the sea level would rise approximately 230 ft (70 m) worldwide.

Glaciers begin when the annual snowfall in a region far exceeds the amount of snow and ice that melts in a given summer. Gravity then causes them to flow outwards and downwards under the pressure of their own weight. Accumulating water and all kinds of sediment (boulders, cobbles, pebbles, sand, silt, and clay) they move very slowly. Great quantities of material accumulate in relatively short periods of geologic time. This mass will continue to grow under similar climatic conditions.

In addition to snow, ice, sediment, and water, glaciers also contain what is called firn or partly compressed snow. During its movement down a mountain, usually toward the ocean, the ice cracks. These cracks are called crevasses. At depth snow is transformed into ice due to compaction of the overlying snow and the refreezing of melted water. When ablation (i.e. melting or calving at the waterline) exceeds the rate of flow the glacier will begin to terminate. This process is evident in many of the glaciers in Patagonia.

CLIMATE and WEATHER

An early description of the weather in western Patagonia (Pacific Coast) is found in the *Proceedings of the 1830 English Expedition*:

> *The climate of Western Patagonia is so disagreeable that the country is almost uninhabitable. Clouds, wind, and rain are continual in their annoyance. Perhaps there are not ten days in the year on which rain does not fall; and not thirty on which the wind does not blow strongly; yet the air is mild, and the temperature surprisingly uniform throughout the year. The country is like the worst part of Tierra del Fuego— a range of mountains, half sunk in the ocean; barren to seaward, impenetrably wooded towards the mainland, and always drenched with the waters of fre-*

*quent rain, which are never dried up
by evaporation before fresh showers
fall.*

Actually, the weather is not that bad, but it does vary considerably even in the same day.

There are three geographic zones in *Isla Grande* (another name for Tierra del Fuego): a plain with rolling hills and waterways, forests in the central part, and a mountain zone. In the plains the average temperature is 41°F (5°C) with 15 in (380 mm) average annual rainfall. The mountains and central zone have much more humid weather with frequent rain and snow. The winds, usually from the southwest or west, are on average about 19 mph (30 kph). However, it's true that the climate of Tierra del Fuego is surprisingly moderate. It is neither very cold in winter nor very hot in summer. In the northeast part of the island the average temperature is said to be about 50° F (10° C) with rare extremes of 81° F (27° C) and 3°F (–16°C). In the cordilleran region (which includes Ushuaia), at sea level, the annual average is about 41° F (5° C) with rare extremes of 84° F (29°C) and –6°F (–21°C).

Precipitation varies more markedly than does temperature. From 180 in (460 cm) at Bahía Félix on Isla Desolación, Chile, to 20 in (51 cm) at Río Grande, Argentina and, in the northern part of Patagonia, annual rainfall is about 110 in (280 cm).

On the central part of the more southern Beagle Channel the rainfall rises to some 217 in (550 cm). The western part of Tierra del Fuego may get 80 in (200 cm) and the Pacific entrance to the Strait of Magellan nearly 20 ft (6 m)! The eastern (Atlantic) mouth of the Strait gets only about 10 in (250 mm). Punta Arenas is quite similar to Santiago at 17 in (430 mm).

In some areas the precipitation drops off drastically over a short distance. There are places where the change from rainforest to almost desert occurs within only 6 mi (10 km). Perhaps nowhere else on earth do precipitation levels drop so dramatically.

The unpredictability of the weather is due to the strong maritime influence. The severe winds (the williwaws) are caused by the strong low-pressure systems that build up over the Argentine steppes in the summer from the sun's warming effect. Moist air from the Pacific rushes into the low-pressure system. Winds are strongest during the summer, with the winter air being almost still. The wind is almost always from the west, which explains, to some extent, the difficulty that the old sailing ships had getting from the Atlantic to the Pacific.

The Southern hemisphere is not simply a mirror image of the Northern hemisphere when it comes to climate and length of daylight. Due to the peculiarities of the earth's rotation Punta Arenas, Chile and Manchester, England, at almost exactly the same latitudes in the two hemispheres, actually experience different lengths of daylight. Punta Arenas has more summer daylight and less winter daylight than does Manchester. Summer days are long, so you may find yourself having dinner in the sunlight. A summer day will last for seventeen and a half hours, while a winter day will be only seven hours long.

The coldest months are July and August with the warmest being January and February. In other words, the seasons are reversed from what they are in the northern hemisphere. The fact that more of the southern hemisphere is ocean (about 80%) means that the southern lands tend to be more temperate.

There isn't as much snow as one would expect, except for the mountains and glaciers. As is true of everything else about the weather here, the amount of snowfall depends on where in Patagonia you are. In one valley, for example, there is usually snow from May to October—and there can be a 6 $1/2$ ft (2 m) accumulation at a time.

In Patagonia many days are cloudy with intermittent rain, but there are also some bright sunny days. More unusual than the temperature, rain, or cloudiness, of course, is the wind. The windiest period of the year is from September to March. Technically, a williwaw occurs in the mountains, but the term also applies to squalls on the water. The williwaw may come down from a mountain or through a valley with a great deal of noise. It may be accompanied by rain or hail, but it is sure to be over soon. Kayakers on the lakes of Torres del Paine Park fear these.

The ocean here is cold. Temperature on the surface is in the range of 41 to 44°F (5 to 7°C) with ice floes in many places. The water itself does not freeze except in some lakes in Tierra del Fuego fed by fresh water. Although the ocean consists of salt water its salinity is low because of the cold temperature. The ocean is also dark. That is because the channels are deep and the sunlight is so often obscured by clouds.

To the traveler tides are not a major factor. They may not even be noticed. (Of course if you are a ship's captain that's another story). The tidal extremes decrease from north to south.

There is one tidal effect that is sometimes observable. In the Beagle Channel the tide runs predominantly from west to east. Near the eastern mouth, though, it runs from east to west. This means that the two tides clash almost in front of Puerto Williams. If you should be there at the right time on the *Terra Australis* you might ask the ship's captain to point out this phenomenon. He is a genial, friendly man who likes to explain things to passengers.

The predominant current in the area is the Austral Pacific current which runs from west to east. It divides on the western coast of South America, the northern part being the Humboldt Current that runs north along the coast of Chile and Peru. The southern branch, the Cape Horn Current, flows around Tierra del Fuego.

ANIMALS

Guanaco

Probably the most commonly seen, and certainly the most interesting, of the wild mammals in Patagonia is the guanaco (gwa-NA-co). It is one of the four South American camelids, the others being the llama, the alpaca, and the vicuna. The llama and the guanaco are the larger of the four while the alpaca and the vicuna have more wool. The guanaco is somewhat smaller than the llama, but they are otherwise very similar. The guanaco's ears are shaped differently than the llama's ears. All guanacos have a similar color pattern, although the intensity of the pattern varies with the region.

The guanaco is brown and white with the upper body, neck, and the fronts of the limbs colored brown. The backs of the limbs, chest, belly, and anal region are whitish to cream, with the white area usually extending quite high into the flanks, as high as the point of the hip. Normally the head is greyish to black. The guanaco has a long neck and small head. This humpless animal is very agile and is a fast runner. Guanacos live in herds, on the plains during the winter, and in the mountains during the summer.

M/V Terra Australis

© Craig Sholley/International Expeditions, Inc.

Patagonia

© International Expeditions, Inc.

Mountain at sunset

Photo by Dick Lutz

Ice floes in Torres del Paine National Park

Photo by Mary Lutz

Torres del Paine

Guanacos

Photo by Mary Lutz

Penguins on Magdalena Island

Photo by Mary Lutz

The llama has been widely domesticated and is seen commonly in Chile, Peru, and other South American countries. In recent years it has become a favorite animal for show, backpacking, and other uses in the United States. The alpaca and vicuna are less common but have also been domesticated, primarily for their wool. The guanaco is probably the most abundant of the four camelids. It is believed that llamas were domesticated from the guanaco, probably around 4000 BC.

The guanaco, on the other hand, has seldom been domesticated in modern times, but there are three guanaco farms in existence–two in South America and one in Wales. Baby guanacos are called *chulengos,* born one at a time in late spring or early summer (November to January). Chulengos have an eighty-percent mortality rate, as they are a favorite meal of the puma. Male guanaco live in all-male herds from about one year of age. They eventually become territorial and attract females to their territory. Families consist of one adult male and four to twelve females and their offspring.

While traveling through the barren parts of Patagonia, you can frequently see lone guanaco standing like sentinels on a hilltop. It's easy to imagine that they are serving as lookouts for their harems, but that is not the case. They are actually sentries for the other males in their territory.

Antonio Pigafetta, the chronicler of Magellan's voyage, described the guanaco as having "the head and the ears of a mule, the body of a camel, the legs of a deer, and the tail and squeals of a horse." Although written nearly five centuries ago this is still a surprisingly accurate description.

Full-grown male guanacos weigh about 200 lbs (91 kg) and stand about 43 in (110 cm). Their habitat ranges all the way from near the equator to Cape Horn, particularly in the high grasslands of the Andes.

Males will defend their feeding territories and fight for females by kicking, biting, pushing, and spitting at each other. The losers wander alone or stick to all-male groups. The animals are hunted for meat, particularly in Argentina, but they are protected in Torres del Paine National Park in Chile so the numbers there are increasing.

An environment vs. economy conflict has developed over the years. In sheep farming areas, the guanacos are considered nuisances because they compete with the sheep for food and water. It is reported, though, that guanaco meat is in the diet of some of the few people living in the drier areas of Argentine Patagonia.

William Conway, the president of the Wildlife Conservation Society, has noted: "Guanacos are a marvelous part of wild Patagonia. No other animal so well conveys the ambiance of its steppes and the lands near its shores."

It has been estimated that the guanaco population of southern South America was 30 to 50 million when Europeans arrived in the 1500s. Today about 575,000 guanaco remain, mostly in Argentina. CITES, the Convention on International Trade in Endangered Species, classifies the guanaco as Appendix II, which means it can be managed for limited use. The animal continues to be a survivor. It adapts to a variety of diets and terrain. Chile, in particular, is working on guanaco conservation, planning to utilize it efficiently for meat and wool production.

The guanaco was declared a protected species in 1929. However, the population is still declining, particularly in Argentina. Chile has done a better job of protection; the population of guanacos has actually increased on both Tierra del Fuego and in Torres del Paine National Park. The classification as vulnerable or endangered has been lifted in the Chilean part of Tierra del Fuego.

The guanacos in Torres del Paine have become less wild, which means curious travelers can get within 50 ft (15 m) or so and easily take excellent photographs. Elsewhere in Patagonia guanacos can be seen only at a distance.

Guanaco meat is much like lean, tasty beef; the wool is considered to be excellent in quality. But guanaco farming itself is not very popular, although it is being tried. One of the problems is that the shearing of a guanaco results in only about one-eighth as much wool as from the shearing of a sheep. In addition, the animals are not as easily managed as sheep or cattle. One solution that is being tried is the cross-breeding of guanacos with alpacas.

A story is told that when sheep were first introduced to Patagonia by Europeans, the natives considered sheep to be "white guanacos" and hunted them as they had always hunted the wild guanaco. One can imagine that the docile sheep were much easier game than the wily guanaco. Not surprisingly this outraged the settlers, who began hunting and killing the Indians.

The Indians utilized guanaco pelts and meat over the years. On this trip you will see in museums examples of the *quillango*, a poncho-like garment that was made and used by the Indians. Traditionally this was constructed from the pelts of thirteen guanacos and therefore a much-prized possession.

The Indians also used to capture the *chulengos* (young guanacos) soon after they were born and raise them as pets.

To many of the groups of Indians in Patagonia, the guanaco was a part of daily life–a very important cultural artifact as well as an economic resource. For the Tehuelches and Onas, especially, the guanaco was pervasive in their myths and stories. The animals were hunted using bows and arrows, spears, and bolas. Sometimes the natives used dogs in their hunting and, later, horses. (Horses were introduced by the Spanish in the sixteenth century). The guanacos provided not only meat for food, and hides for clothing, but also bones for tools, internal organs for medicines, and sinews for sewing. In fact, the Ona were nearly totally dependent on guanacos for their very existence. Today's hunters, with the exception of the occasional poacher, have little interest in the guanaco, because they have no horns or antlers to serve as trophies. If the population density in Patagonia were anywhere near as high as in North America or Europe, the animals would probably be hunted similarly to deer. The law in the Chilean part of Tierra del Fuego does allow for the capture and release of wild guanacos for the purpose of harvesting their wool.

You will probably not find guanaco meat on a restaurant menu in Patagonia, but you might find it occasionally in other parts of the world, as there is a small amount exported as game meat. The dried meat or jerky (*charqui*) is common in certain parts of South America, particularly where lack of refrigeration is common. Guanaco wool is extremely fine and, consequently, quite valuable. With a minimum of processing it sells for approximately $150 a pound ($320 a kilogram). At least, this is the price in Wales.

The guanaco is a handsome, interesting animal that has provided many benefits to native groups in the past. Wild populations remain well protected so the utilization of domesticated guanacos is expected to be a significant industry for Patagonia in the future.

Huemul

An animal you might see is the rare huemel. This deer, along with the condor, appears on Chile's national emblem. The huemul, which reaches one meter in height, weighs 100 to 140 lb (45 to 65 kg), and is strong and agile. This animal is also known as the South Andean deer. In the summer it grazes at higher altitudes, moves down the mountains in the fall, and spends the winter in forested valleys. It feeds primarily on herbaceous plants and shrubs.

Hunting, habitat loss because of fire and erosion, and the competition from the red deer are some of the causes for its population decline. There may be only a couple of thousand of them left.

Puma

It's the same animal which is elsewhere known as the cougar, mountain lion, or panther. Except for man, the puma is found over a wider range than any other mammal in the western hemisphere, roaming all the way from southern British Columbia to Patagonia. A male may grow up to 6 ft (1.8 m) with its tail adding an additional 2–3 ft (60–90 cm). It may weigh as much as 200 lb (91 kg). Its life expectancy in the wild is about twelve years.

Most active at dusk or dawn, pumas hunt at any time of the day or night. They eat a variety of food but in Patagonia they feed mainly on guanaco. It is suspected that they have contributed to the virtual disappearance of the huemel as well. They take sheep and cattle also. Pumas are protected in Torres del Paine National Park and are occasionally seen there. (Guanacos are protected from man, but not from puma). They may breed at any time of the year. If you hear a blood-curdling scream while visiting Torres del Paine it may be a female advertising that she is in season. Young puma are usually born every other year in litters of one to five young. The kittens have spotted coats until they are about six months old. Able to hunt for themselves after nine months, they will remain with their mother for two years. In late spring or summer they may start to become independent of their mothers by attempting to find a home range of their own. It is at this time that they are most likely to be observed by humans.

Pumas normally do not attack humans, and are rarely a problem n a sparsely populated area like Patagonia.

Fox

There are two species of fox in Patagonia, particularly in Torres del Paine National Park. The more common type is the South American grey fox, which, like the guanaco, is not as shy around humans as its counterpart in other areas. The animals seem to know that they are protected and will not be harmed. This is not to imply that they are exactly tame, but the foxes and the guanacos are easily photographable.

The male grey fox weighs up to about 9 lb (4 kg) and stands about 16 in (40 cm) high at the shoulder. This animal is omnivorous, surviving on birds, small mammals such as hares and mice, frogs, lizards, beetles, scorpions, other insects, and even berries. Also it occasionally dines on the remains of a puma-killed guanaco.

Grey foxes form family units, and young are born in the spring. The litters may contain as many as six pups.

Another more shy fox is the red fox, which is considerably larger than the grey. The red fox, or "colored fox" weighs about 27 lb (12 kg) and measures 39 to 42 in (100 to 107 cm). The red fox is carnivorous, surviving on a diet of lizards, birds, rodents, and sheep.

Interestingly the two species of fox have different territories and never overlap. The grey fox is much more adaptable and survives in a poorer environment than its larger cousin.

Both the grey and the red fox are members of a different genus than the North American foxes. They descended from a more wolf-like lineage about seven million years ago before migrating across the Isthmus of Panama.

Beaver

A very common animal in southern Patagonia is one that isn't native. It's the American beaver, which was introduced in the 1940s to the area. The Argentine government brought twenty-five pairs of beavers from Canada to Tierra del Fuego in hopes of establishing a fur industry. When the project failed, they released the beavers. The officials neglected to consider the fact that Tierra del Fuego contains no natural predators of the beaver. There were no wolves or bears, as there were in Canada. In an effort to control their population, foxes and eagles were introduced. These predators soon began eating other types of wildlife, however, and this has contributed to the continued explosion in the beaver population.

That original fifty beavers may now have multiplied to as many as 100,000! Paying no attention to national borders, they have expanded into the Chilean section of Tierra del Fuego. As a matter of fact there are probably more beavers on the Chilean side than on the Argentine because the Argentinians have done more hunting and trapping. The animals also have swum to some outlying islands and scientists fear that they will establish a foothold on the South American mainland. (This may already have occurred.)

Beavers cause a great deal of damage to the ecosystem. They cut down trees and dam rivers to create lakes. The lakes, in turn, flood forestland and some of the few roads, threatening the very livelihood of local residents. Can you imagine what they will do to the Andean forests if they ever reach the mainland?

Beavers are rodents, but perhaps due to their industriousness, they have a good reputation. Animal rights advocates do not object to rat eradication campaigns, but beavers are different. The Argentine government has attempted to persuade the European Community to open its market to Argentine beaver pelts in an effort to encourage trapping of the troublesome rodents. The EC does allow the import of beaver pelts, but only if the animals have been caught in traps that immediately kill their prey.

The government has since trained trappers in acceptable techniques and has provided Canadian-designed traps to many trappers. These traps are acceptable to the European Community officials but they object to the fact that other types of traps are allowed elsewhere in Argentina.

These "restraining" traps are used widely in the trapping of other animals whose pelts can be exported without difficulty. Therefore Argentina is reluctant to comply with the EC's demands.

This bureaucratic maneuvering may not be relevant, since the overall demand for fur pelts has been drastically reduced in the world. In the meantime, beavers proceed with their destructive campaign despite the best efforts of governments.

It is said that beavers are second only to man in their ability to alter the landscape. An adult beaver may weigh up to 40 lb (18 kg). They mate for life during their third year and bear young in the spring. There are usually one to four in each litter. The young stay with their parents for two years and act as babysitters for the new litter. Although beavers have a small brain they do learn by imitation and experience. An intriguing fact is that the European beaver, almost identical in many ways to the American beaver, does not have any interest in dam construction. Instead it digs burrows in stream banks.

In the long run, beavers will naturally limit their own population to a sustainable level. Thus, although beavers will probably continue to wreak havoc on the forests of Tierra del Fuego, their population will be controlled by the amount of food available.

Patagonian Cavy

The Patagonian cavy or *mara* looks like a rabbit but is really a guinea pig. It lives in arid regions of the northern part of Patagonia, mostly in Argentina. It reaches a length of about $2\,1/2$ ft (76 cm) and weighs about 15 to 20 lb (7 to 9 kg). Living on herbs and grasses, its body is that of a long-legged rodent but has some similarity to a hoofed animal. The mara is monogamous for life, with a pair breeding two or three times a year, usually around mid-winter and spring. One to three young are born after a three-month gestation period. They are placed in a communal den, usually made from a hole or tunnel abandoned by another animal. This den is home to as many as fifteen cavy pairs and their young. In some ways, the cavy's lifestyle is similar to that of the prairie dog. Weaned after two to three months the young quickly reach sexual maturity (two to three months for females, six months for males).

The animals travel in various ways, sometimes walking, sometimes hopping like a rabbit, galloping, or bouncing on all fours (for long-distance, high-speed travel). Cavies have been clocked at speeds of 45 kph (28 mph) for more than 1,000 m (1,093 yd.) They can not only run fast, but they jump high when alarmed. Not surprisingly, they handle extremely cold weather well.

Orca

Occasionally seen in Patagonia is an Orca or killer whale. Technically, these are not actually whales but the largest member of the group of marine mammals known as dolphins. Killer whales were originally called 'whale killers' by Spanish whalers. They grow up to about 27 ft (8 m) in length and can weigh up to 10 tons. They are black with white patches. Orcas have an average of twenty-four sharp, conical, and slightly curved teeth. They eat other whales, fishes, birds (including penguins), seals, sea lions, and squid. They have no natural predators other than each other and, of course, man.

Although found in all oceans from the tropics to the poles this fierce ocean hunter tends toward cooler water. Hunting of killer whales has been banned by the International Whaling Commission.

Killers often hunt in small packs of up to twenty individuals while using their "calls" to organize and coordinate their hunts. Sometimes they can be found living alone.

Easily spotted from a distance they have distinctive black triangle-shaped back fins. The males are bigger than the females and have dorsal fins standing straight up for about 6 ft (2 m). The dorsal fins of females, on the other hand, stand up only about 3 ft (1 m) and are sickle-shaped. The newborn calves are nearly 7 ft (2 m) in length and weigh almost 400 lb (180 kg) at birth. Scientists believe that males live seventy to eighty years and females live on average about fifty years. There are some reports of females living over a hundred years.

Southern Right Whale

The whale you're most likely to see around Patagonia is the Southern right whale. It is a medium-sized whale attaining lengths up to 15m (49 ft) and weighing up to 60tons.

Right whales are stocky (short and fat) and black. You can recognize them by the fact that they have no dorsal fin. They also sport a highly arched jaw, and have growths on their head called callosities.These white gr owths also appear on the lower jaw and around the eye. These are unique to each whale and provide an easy means of identification. The tail is broad and smooth and divided by a deep notch. The tail is often lifted out of the water as the animal dives.

They live and breed in herds in coastal waters and in bays, though they spend a lot of time in the open ocean. They are an endangered species; there still aren't very many of them despite the fact that commercial hunting stopped many years ago. They can migrate up to 5,000 km (3,100 mi) being found at times off the coasts of Australia and South Africa.

They acquired the name "right whales" because they were slow and easy to catch, so the whalers considered them the "right whales" to hunt! They also float when they die whereas many whales do not.

Like all baleen whales they filter their food through their long baleen plates. They feed by simply opening their mouths and grazing along the surface of the water for plankton.

The right whale mates at about eight years of age. The gestation period is about thirteen months, and the females can give birth every three to five years.

Scientists estimate that right whales live at least fifty years. They are sometimes preyed upon by killer whales.

Southern Elephant Seal

The Southern elephant seal, (technically a pinniped) is sometimes called a "sea elephant." A huge four-ton beast with a stout squared-off head, a small trunk-like nose, and flippers, these creatures will almost certainly be seen on the International Expeditions trip. The males (called bulls) use their trunks to fight for breeding rights. The bulls may be as much as three times as big as the females (called cows). These mammals are excellent swimmers but aren't very maneuverable on land.

Growing to over twenty feet long, the elephant seal is the largest member of the seal family. The Northern elephant seal lives off the coast of California and Baja California while the Southern elephant seal lives on the rocky shores of the Antarctic Islands and Patagonia. The Northern elephant seal is yellowish or gray-brown, while the Southern is blue-gray. The southern species molts a considerable amount of hair and skin. Unlike the northern species the Southern elephant seal winters at sea, possibly near the pack ice.

The elephant seal's diet consists of large fish, squid, and an occasional penguin. Bulls that have a harem of females are called "beachmasters."

They may have a harem of fifty cows! Cows produce pups yearly after an eleven-month gestation period.

These beasts were formerly extensively hunted for their oil, and in the nineteenth century were reduced almost to extinction. Now protected, they have gradually increased in number and are no longer considered threatened. Elephant seals are gregarious animals but during the breeding season the males become aggressive toward each other.

Southern Fur Seal

The Southern fur seal is known as the "eared seal" due to its external ear flaps. These seals stand with the fore and hind limbs under the body, pointing forward. Males weigh between 130 and 265 lb (60 and 120 kg) and females weigh between 66 and 112 lb (30 and 51 kg.) Adult males are 3 to 6 ft (1 to 2 m) long, and females are 1 $^{1}/_{2}$ ft to 3 ft ($^{1}/_{2}$ to 1 m.)

Adult Southern fur seals have a dense velvety underpelt, which is both waterproof and windproof, and an outer layer of coarse grey-brown hair. The males have a long mane of shoulder fur, the females do not. Babies are born with black wooly fur, which is retained for 2–3 months until they display a silver-grey coat that lasts until adulthood.

The animal's diet is mainly krill, but individuals also consume squids and even birds. They usually feed at night in the shallower waters of the ocean.

The breeding season is from November to January. Breeding takes place on rocky beaches sheltered from the sea. The males come first to the breeding grounds to compete for territories. The individual fur seal's harem will eventually hold four or five females. Competition for females is fierce, so males don't even feed while defending their territories on shore. This results in the male losing an average of 3 $^{1}/_{3}$ lb (1 $^{1}/_{2}$ kg) a day throughout the season. Some males who lose out in the fight for females are forced inland while others assume a completely aquatic lifestyle.

A single young is born approximately two days after the mother's arrival on shore. Probably due to the harsh weather conditions, the lactation period is one of the shortest of all fur seals.

The Southern fur seal is surprising agile on land, reaching speeds of 12 mph (20 kph) on smooth surfaces. Probably they reach even higher speeds in the water.

The Southern fur seal (also known as the Antarctic fur seal) is no longer of economic importance to humans, but throughout the eighteenth and nineteenth centuries the species was heavily hunted for its fur. Today the fur is considered too coarse for commercial markets. Southern fur seals are now growing at the rate of about ten percent per year.

Commercial harvesting of krill for human consumption is now being developed in some countries. This threatens another battle between human interests and those of the seal, this time over who gets the krill. The Southern fur seal is protected under the Convention for Conservation of Antarctic Seals (CCAS) and the Antarctic Treaty as well as by the nations involved. They are on Appendix II of the Convention on International Trade in Endangered Species (CITES.)

Southern Sea Lion

The Southern sea lion (also known as the South American sea lion) can be distinguished from the Southern fur seal in many ways. The sea lion does not have the external ear characteristic of the fur seal, and it is considerably bigger, with adult males ranging from 6 to 8 ft (2 to 2 $^1/_2$ m) in length and weighing from 440 to 770 lb (200 to 350 kg). Females average 6 ft (2 m) in length and weigh from 310 to 330 lb (140 to 150 kg), less than half the average weight of an adult male.

The male lion's coat is dark brown on the back and dark yellow to gold on the belly. Males have a full mane, which is a paler color than the coat. A male's posture is usually upright. The female's coat is lighter in color than the male's, varying from a fair brown to yellow with some pale markings around the head.

Southern sea lions are carnivorous. Their diet includes fish, cephalopods, crustaceans, and other invertebrates depending on local abundance. They hunt in shallow waters, not more than five miles from shore. They hunt in groups. After catching a fish, they usually shake the fish in the air and often eat it whole. Males have been observed eating penguins and female fur seals and their pups. They have been known to steal fish by following fishing boats and stealing fish from the nets.

Southern sea lions are social animals that live in groups. These groups usually consist of several females and one or more males. The males patrol their territory and threaten intruders. They advertise their territorial boundaries through vocalizations.

Males begin, from early August to December, to defend their territories aggressively and to show interest in females. Their mating behavior includes making noise, rubbing noses, smelling, playful biting, and mouth contact. Usual breeding grounds are on beaches of sand, pebbles, or flat rock. Males keep females from leaving the area until they have mated.

The gestation period is about a year with young born from mid-December to early February in the year after mating. Usually one pup is born at a time.

Within a few days after giving birth females mate again with the male in their territory. The female then leaves her pup behind to go to sea to find food. She returns from her sea trips at intervals to nurse her young. The mothers locate their pup by first calling to it and then identifying it by smell. Occasionally mothers are unable to find their pup. This may be the result of high tides, storms, or male abductions.

Sometimes, particularly in larger populations, pups are trampled to death by adult sea lions. Pups usually go into the water for the first time at about three to four weeks of age. They enter in a large group with other sea lions. They nurse for about six to twelve months, until the following year when the mother gives birth to another pup. Mothers have been known to nurse both pups simultaneously.

Sometimes groups of males raid the families, abducting and occasionally killing the pups. Mothers do not usually resist or try to retrieve the abducted pup. The males are so much bigger than the females that resistance is futile.

Fights are not common but occasionally occur between two bulls at the beginning of the breeding season. The more females in heat, the more fights. Bulls grunt and attack each other by biting and tearing. Frequently pups are stepped on and killed. Bulls may keep their territories for two to three mating seasons until another bull takes over.

Males mature at six years while females reach maturity at four years. Typically a male will have eighteen cows in his territory. The young males who have not obtained females usually live with other young males in groups of ten to forty. They will raid other territories in order to obtain females.

In addition to shorelines and beaches Southern sea lions reside along flat rocky shelves or cliffs with tidepools and boulders. An interesting feature of sea lions is their reaction to extremes of temperature. When it gets too cold, sea lions will position their body so that as little surface area of the body as possible is exposed to the air. They lay on their belly and cover their forepaws. When it gets too warm, they lie on their backs with one hindfoot projected outwards.

Until recently they were hunted for their fur, meat, and oil but are now protected throughout most of the world. They are not considered threatened. The average lifespan of Southern sea lions is sixteen to twenty years. One lived in captivity for almost twenty-five years. Sharks and killer whales are among their predators.

BIRDS

Andean Condor

The Andean condor weighs 20 to 25 lb (9 to 11 kg) and is 40 to 46 in (102 to 117 cm) long. With a wingspan of over ten feet, the Andean condor is considered by most to be the largest flying bird in the world. Found in Patagonia, it

ranges as far north as Venezuela. Condors must
have thermals (rising warm air currents) in order to maintain their flight. Thus, they live in the
mountains. In Patagonia, though, they are sometimes found on shorelines.

Andean condors eat mostly dead animals
which they locate by sight, but they also have a
highly developed sense of smell. They may travel
over many hundreds of miles in search of food.
A significant part of their diet in Patagonia consists of dead sea lion pups. They sometimes kill
an animal, but they are not really built to kill.
Their claws are not as sharp as other birds of prey.
Their hooked beak is best for tearing meat. Large
carrion may not be totally eaten for several days
because their eyes are bigger than their stomach.
They feed on the ground, as they are unable to
carry away their prey. In fact, with this in mind a
local hunting technique is to allow the condor to
gorge itself to the point where it cannot fly away
and then one can easily capture it by hand.

The Andean condor's head is red or blackish
red. The head is bare skin; apparently being without feathers lessens the risk of acquiring bacte-
ria from the carcasses they feed on. The head of
the male has a large, comb-like fleshy crest, loose
folds of skin on the side of the neck, and a two-
inch hanging wattle. (If ugliness is a virtue this
is a very moral beast). The smaller female,
though, does not have the crest or the wattle. The
Andean condor's body is black with some white
on the wings. Both male and female have a

snowy-white neck ruff.

The birds congregate in flocks until breeding season, when the flocks disperse. Courtship rituals include dancing as well as walking back and forth hissing and clucking with their wings held out. Besides the hissing and clucking the bird has no other voice. Young are born from an egg laid on the bare rock of a ledge or cave in a cliff face. Usually only one is laid and only every other year. The egg hatches after fifty-four to fifty-eight days with both parents doing incubation duty. Also, both parents are involved in care of the young.

The young are unable to fly until about six months old. They cannot reproduce until about six years old. The late maturity, combined with low rate and frequency of egg-laying means their reproduction rate is low. Luckily, individuals may live for fifty years, or, in captivity, as long as seventy years.

Their feet are made for walking, although not for grasping prey. An interesting habit of the condor is urinating on its own legs in very hot weather. This keeps their legs cool.

The Andean condor soars at heights up to 15,000 feet. This is unique among birds. The species is near-threatened according to CITES (Convention on International Trade in Endangered Species.) It has been hunted and poisoned by farmers for years. In some areas of the Andes the Andean condor has a religious significance. Also some people value their feathers for decoration and, in some places the killing of the great condor is a proof of manhood.

Actually, in Patagonia they have not been harassed nearly as much as in other parts of South America. The Andean condor is the national bird of Chile and has been part of the national emblem since 1834.

Penguin

On your expedition to Patagonia, you will see hundreds of thousands of penguins. There are sixteen or eighteen different species of penguins (scientists differ) and four of them have been recorded in the Patagonia area. The vast majority of the ones you see will be Magellanic penguins. They stand from 17 to 27 in (43 to 69 cm) in height and weigh 6 $^{1}/_{2}$ to 7 $^{1}/_{2}$ lb (3 to 3 $^{1}/_{2}$ kg). Penguins are very trusting and somewhat curious. Magellanic penguins can be distinguished from other species of penguins by the distinctive white streak over the eyes that goes behind the ears and then under the chin. The chest has a few black spots in a random pattern. The Magellanic penguin is sometimes called the jackass penguin because of the braying sound it makes.

Penguins have a shape that enables them to be extremely agile under water. In addition, they have a waterproof coat of dense feathers and a layer of fat for insulation. Since this layer is relatively thin when compared with seal or whale blubber, feathers are the primary external mechanism whereby penguins regulate heat. Feathers "pocket" air between the skin and the environment, much like insulation works in your house. The fiber glass or foam insulation has many airspaces that trap air, and in the case of penguins, this air is warm.

Their diet consists of fish, squid, and crustaceans. Predators include the Southern sea lion, the Dominican gull, and the giant petrel. Gulls and petrels eat the penguin's chicks and eggs. Penguins spend much of their life in the sea. However, they lay their eggs and raise their chicks on land. Fortunately for them, they have little or no sense of smell. When you visit the crowded penguin rookery on Magdalena Island, it will be clear why this is fortunate for them!

Penguins are very social birds. Not only on land, but also at sea, they swim and feed in groups. The male and the female both exhibit the same color patterns. Magellanic penguins breed from late September to February. Two eggs are laid in September or October with incubation taking thirty to forty-two days. The chicks leave the nest when they are about sixty to seventy days old.

Magellanic penguins complete their breeding by late February. After a postnuptial molt, most leave the breeding areas and migrate northward. The shallow burrows they live in on land protect them from sun and weather. Also it is a simple physical property that the smaller the surface area to volume ratio, the smaller the extent of heat loss. In other words, smaller species of penguins have the largest surface area to volume ratio, so they must live in warmer climates. Larger penguins have the smallest surface area to volume ratio, and thus retain heat easier than the smaller penguins.

The visit to Magdalena Island, home to about 200,000 penguins was for me one of the most awe-inspiring sights of the whole thrill-filled trip!

Lesser Rhea

The flightless lesser rhea, also known as Darwin's rhea, is smaller than the ostrich which it closely resembles. It only occurs in South America–especially in Patagonia, but also in the Andes in Argentina, Chile, Bolivia, and Peru. The bird stands at 36 to 39 in (92 $1/2$ to 100 cm) and weighs 33 to 55 lb (15 to 25 kg). It is flightless although its wings are proportionally larger than the ostriches. Its wings enable it to maneuver quite well when running. Three-toed, it has a strong claw on the end of each wing that is used effectively as a weapon.

The lesser rhea's feathers are smooth and soft, and cover its thighs. Coloring is basically brown with white flecking throughout, though the female is duller and has fewer white spots on the back. The juvenile is even browner than the adults and doesn't have white spots. The adult plumage is acquired in the third or fourth year.

The diet of the lesser rhea is made up of plant matter, including roots, fruits, seeds, and leaves. Some animal matter is also consumed, specifically insects and small vertebrates. Most of its liquid requirements are satisfied by plants and so it drinks little water. It also ingests pebbles. The abundance of vegetation in its habitat means that it generally has enough food all year.

The breeding season varies. Males compete for territory in short fights. When their territory is established, males attempt to attract females into it by running at them quickly with outspread wings. After a male has succeeded in gathering two to twelve females, he then begins a courtship display. This involves various calls while running around the females and shaking his wings. After mating, the male leads the females in a group to the nest, where they lay their eggs in turn. The females then leave, also in a group. After leaving they return every two or three days to deposit more eggs. The eggs are yellowish olive-green, but fade to buff, and average 5 x 3 $1/2$ in (127 x 87 mm). After the laying is over at a particular nest, the female leaves to mate with another male and repeat the cycle.

The male then handles the incubation and chick-rearing. Incubation may continue for 35–40 days. The male is aggressive toward anything that approaches the nest, including females who come to lay more eggs, which means new eggs are often laid just nearby. The male rolls some of these eggs into the nest, but some get left behind.

The rotting eggs attract flies, which become food for the male and the newly hatched chicks. The nest may consist of anywhere from 13 to 30 eggs. When the first chick in a nest hatches, it begins calling, encouraging the others to hatch. Thus they are all hatched in a period of 24–28 hours.

The male leads the chicks away from the nest after a few days, and they keep in touch by whistling. The male is very protective. Sometimes lost chicks are adopted by another male, which leads to a wide range of ages within one group. The male cares for its young until it is about six months old; then juveniles usually stay in the groups until they are sexually mature at two or three years.

A social animal, the Lesser rhea lives in groups of five to thirty individuals of all ages and both sexes. During the breeding season, males become territorial while females break off into small groups. Sometimes males of advanced age live alone.

The running birds may reach speeds of 37 mph (60 kph). They are good swimmers and have been observed crossing rivers. They have excellent eyesight and hearing. Despite the fact that the rhea can easily outrun predators, this bird has the odd habit of retracing its steps when being pursued, and then suddenly squatting down in the bushes, and flattening its body against the ground. Despite its large size, it can successfully hide in this manner. Another tactic used to confuse predators is to run in a zigzag pattern, or to turn sharply at right angles. Although fast, the rhea doesn't run very far. It is usually active during the daytime.

Sometimes a rhea will feed with other herbivores. This is helpful for both parties because the rhea has good eyesight but a poor sense of smell, while other herbivores have poor eyesight but a keen sense of smell. Thus, together they can better be on the lookout for predators than either can alone. The rheas' habit of wandering around with cattle can be beneficial to farmers, because they eat the burr-like seeds that become entangled in sheep's wool.

The rhea lives in a rather arid habitat such as grassland or savanna. When it comes breeding time, though, it prefers to be near a lake, river, or swamp.

The meat is eaten locally; and the possibility of raising the birds as commercial livestock has been the subject of experiments. Some parts are used for medicine, and the feathers are sold commercially. The skin is used for rugs. The toes of the lesser rhea are considered good luck charms by local people.

Although considered endangered, the rhea is still hunted and its habitat is being destroyed by agriculture. In some mining areas they are hunted from jeeps. They live about twenty years in the wild, and forty in captivity.

Since there is a Lesser rhea, it follows that there is also a greater rhea. It inhabits grassy plains from Bolivia and Brazil to central Argentina. The lesser rhea is found in the high plateau region of the southern Andes and in grasslands south of the range of the greater rhea. The Lesser rhea is found in many parts of Patagonia.

Cormorant

These diving birds are found in various regions of the world.

There are five types of cormorants found in Patagonia; the king cormorant and the rock cormorant being the most common.

King cormorants breed in dense colonies on gentle cliff-top slopes. Nests are constructed from mud and vegetation, with two to four eggs being laid around November. Eggs hatch in December, and chicks remain in the nest until they fledge in February. Their length is 30 in (75 cm). Adults travel long distances in search of schools of small fish and crustaceans, which they catch in flocks during shallow dives.

Rock cormorants, although slightly smaller, have many of the same attributes of the King cormorants but can easily be distinguished. Both birds have white bellies but the Rock has a dark neck whereas the King's white belly continues up its underbody to its neck and chin.

Cormorants lay two to six eggs per clutch. The young are born blind, and the parents feed the nestlings with half-digested food which is dropped into the nests. Later, the young birds poke their heads into the gullet of the adults to feed. Cormorants are long-lived; one is known to have lived eighteen years.

Kelp Gull

Perhaps the most common flying bird in Patagonia, the kelp gull is found primarily along the southern reaches of Tierra del Fuego.

Usually found in large flocks it is very noisy and aggressive when competing for food. The largest of the three types of gulls in the area, it is about 2 ft (61 cm) long. The kelp gull is primarily white with black on its back, sides, and tail.

Turkey Vulture

About half the size of the condor, but like the condor it is a scavenger that frequently soars high in the air. The turkey vulture gets its name from the resemblance of its bald, red head to that of the turkey. Most often seen in flight, it is identified by its two-tone wing color (black in front with trailing grayish-black). Although vultures are scavengers that feed on dead animals, they actually prefer fresh food. When looking for carrion, the turkey vulture relies on its excellent vision and acute sense of smell.

Flamingo

Although known as a tropical bird, the flamingo also is a migratory bird, and can be seen periodically in the Torres del Paine area and near Porvenir. They frequent low-lying brackish water with abundant organic material. They do not nest in the region. The Chilean flamingo is a delicate pink with black on the rear edges of its wings.

Caracara

The striated caracara is heavily-built and blackish-brown in color. This is an impressive bird. It is 24 $1/2$ inches (62 cm) long. It is a scavenger, and also eats the eggs of other seabirds and steals their prey.

The crested caracara is probably the most common bird of prey in the region. It has a black crown that results in its name. Otherwise its color varies from beige to white to dark brown. The crested caracara is 22 in (56 cm) long and is a scavenger and a pirate, but it also preys on small rodents.

The white-throated caracara is somewhat smaller than the other caracaras. This bird has its upper parts black, with the white extending from the throat, down the chest, and to the tail. Feeding habits are much the same as the crested caracara, but it can be seen soaring.

Swan

The coscoroba swan is normally seen in pairs. This white swan can be found from August to May in marshes, lakes, and ponds.

The black-necked swan is an aquatic bird, easily spied near Puerto Natales, but it is also found elsewhere in Patagonia. It is all-white except for its black head and neck.

Austral Parakeet

One of the many amazing discoveries about Patagonia is that there is a tropical parakeet living here. The Austral parakeet looks like it belongs in the rain forest. It is green overall, with a somewhat red forehead. About 14 in (36 cm) long, it is a noisy, gregarious bird that lives in flocks. Several were spotted in the trees in Torres del Paine, but others were sighted by our group on the southern part of Tierra del Fuego (near Ushuaia) and on Navarino Island (near Puerto Williams).

Flightless Steamer Duck

Another remarkable Patagonian bird is the flightless steamer duck. Seen primarily in the Beagle Channel, it is the biggest duck in the region, measuring 31 $1/2$ in (80 cm) long. It is mostly gray with an orange bill. Despite not being very colorful, it is a bird you will want to see. This is because of the way it races through the water. Entirely unable to fly it moves from place to place by whirling its wings like paddles in what appears to be desperation. It reminds me of a Mississippi paddle-wheeler. There is also a flying steamer duck in Patagonia.

Other Birds

There are many other species of birds in Patagonia: grebes, albatrosses, geese, hawks, and more. Several of the species represented live only in Patagonia. Our group saw more species here in Patagonia than our International Expeditions' trip did in the Amazon (see *Hidden Amazon* by Dick Lutz). I had no idea that Patagonia was such a birdwatcher's paradise.

Drake's expedition was actually driven from a Patagonian island by the weight and aggressiveness of the multitude of birds. The incident is described thus:

> *...every third bird could not find any room, in so much that they sought to settle themselves upon our heads and shoulders, arms, and all parts of our body they could in strange manner, without any fear; yea they were so speedy to place themselves upon us, that one of us was glad to help another,*

*and when no beating with poles, cud-
gels, swords, and daggers would keep
them off from our bodies, we were
driven with our hands to pull them
away from another, till with pulling
and killing we fainted.*

FLORA

Calafate

Perhaps the best-known plant of Patagonia
is the *calafate*, a blue berry that grows on a shrub
which may grow up to 10 ft (3 m) high. The
calafate has a delicious flavor and has long been
a staple for explorers, Indians, and animals. There
is a local saying that whoever eats the calafate
berry will return to this land. The berry is made
into a jam that is available in souvenir shops. It
grows on the steppe and shrubland areas as well
as in clearings and on the edge of forests.

Beech Trees

One of the most common trees in Patagonia
is the *lenga*. A deciduous tree (and sometimes a
shrub), the lenga grows to 100 ft (30 m) high. One
of three varieties of beech found in the area, the
lenga grows mainly in eastern Tierra del Fuego
and in Chile north as far as Torres del Paine. Its
leaves are waxy in appearance and about 1 to 1

$1/2$ in (3 to 4 cm) long. The roots of the lenga grow outward rather than down, thus enabling the tree to prosper in only a few centimeters of fertile soil. Its wood is a beautiful hardwood, and when turned into furniture it is almost identical to American black cherry. It matures in seventy to 100 years, and thus the opponents of logging the lenga forests insist that it is unrealistic to expect the lenga to renew itself. There are vast areas of lenga forest in Tierra del Fuego. The commercial harvesting of lenga in Tierra del Fuego is an area of much dispute. (This dispute is dealt with at greater length in Chapter V.)

Another beech tree, also losing its leaves annually, is the *ñirre*. This dwarf species usually has a shrunken appearance with a gnarled and twisted trunk.

The third species of beech is an evergreen called *coigue*. Like the lenga, it can grow up to 100 ft (30 m) tall. Its leaves are similar to the lenga's but lighter in color and less waxy. It usually thrives in a wetter area than the lenga.

Local Variety

As you hike in the region you'll occasionally see wildflowers. Some of the lupine are very tall, perhaps 5 ft (1 $1/2$ cm) but most of the flowers are quite small.

A mesquite-like shrub is commonly seen in the steppe areas of Patagonia.

Peat moss is frequently found in Tierra del Fuego. You will particularly experience it in Tierra del Fuego National Park in Argentina.

III

HISTORY

EXPLORERS

Magellan

The Strait of Magellan was first discovered by Ferdinand Magellan in 1520. Magellan was Portuguese, born sometime between 1475 and 1485. When he reached adulthood, Magellan became a sailor and for seven years roamed the East (primarily India and the Moluccas). Upon returning to Lisbon he proposed to Don Manoel, King of Portugal, that he make a voyage around the world. He planned to go to the south, through some way yet to be discovered, into the South Sea and then westward to the Spice Islands (Moluccas) and homeward around Africa's Cape of Good Hope.

Don Manoel, after listening to his advisors, rejected the proposal. Magellan then moved to Spain, became a Spanish subject, married a Spanish woman, and entered the service of the seventeen-year-old Charles I, King of Spain. King Charles bought into Magellan's scheme.

Another version of what caused Magellan to renounce his Portuguese citizenship and opt for Spain's is that he was denied compensation for a wound he received while fighting for Portugal in Morocco. In a huff he published a formal renunciation of Portuguese citizenship and moved to Spain.

After receiving authorization and funding Magellan began getting ready for the trip. Preparations for the voyage were extensive. More than 400 tons of equipment, supplies, and food stores were distributed among the five ships assigned for the voyage. Magellan proved to be a driver–inspecting each operation, watching the stress on the capstans, supervising the caulking, and the nailing of lead strips along the underwater seams to hold the caulked oakum. Both the preparations and the records of the process were extraordinarily complete. Magellan's was the most thoroughly documented sea voyage up to that time.

Some five years before Magellan set out, a brave navigator named De Solis had embarked on a voyage of discovery only to be killed, roasted, and eaten by cannibals along the Río de la Plata (the site of present-day Buenos Aires, Argentina.) Five of his men were dealt with in the same fashion while the remainder of his crew watched from their ships offshore. They were so appalled that they immediately returned to Spain. The memory of this incident made rounding up enough crew members difficult, but finally the five ships sailed on September 20, 1519.

Over 200 men sailed out on what was later to be deemed the greatest voyage of exploration in the history of the world. Only eighteen men and one ship returned. Fortunately, a detailed record of the voyage was kept. Antonio Pigafetta, an Italian, was the chronicler of the voyage.

Captain-General Magellan (he insisted on being called that) was a stern, and you could say cruel, disciplinarian. After the first part of the voyage–across the south Atlantic–the crew began to mutiny. Dealing with it harshly, Magellan ordered the captain of one of his ships (who was also the King's treasurer) hung, drawn, quartered, and impaled on stakes. This took place in San Julian on the beach. The mutinous officers were beheaded.

Though ruthless as he drove his men toward his objectives, Magellan evidently showed compassion for the sick and an unusual tolerance and understanding when interacting with the natives he encountered.

Remaining in Port San Julian for five months, the ships, now down to four, sailed on August 24, 1520. Easing down the coastline some 200 m (320 km) they came to an opening that led to a strait. Today, the promontory of land there is known as Cape Virgins. The name comes from Cape of the Eleven Thousand Virgins, so named by Magellan. It was discovered on the day of St. Ursula and her Virgins, which was an important religious holiday at the time. St. Ursula, a sixth-century nun, was believed to have had a vision of eleven thousand virgins who confirmed that she would win the battle over the Huns.

Sailing into the strait, the men saw the fires of the natives on the banks to the south. Magellan named this land (which later proved to be a large island) *Tierra del Fuego*, the Land of Fire. With difficulty the four ships maneuvered through this twisting body of water to "The Great South Sea" (Pacific Ocean).

The actual discovery of the Strait of Magellan is an interesting story. When the four ships remaining in the expedition rounded a cape south of St. Julian they came upon a pleasant-appearing horseshoe-shaped bay.

The water in this magnificent bay was a pale aquamarine, which indicated to the sailors that the estuary was shallow. The beaches were of white sand with snow-capped mountains in the distance. Altogether a pleasant scene but it didn't appear that the bay had any outlet, other than the ocean.

Suddenly a storm blew up with two of the ships (including Magellan's) fleeing out to sea. The other two ships of the expedition were caught in the bay and took a horrendous amount of punishment from the violent storm. It seemed as though they were destined to be crushed upon the rocks.

After the storm calmed down the two ships that had gone to sea returned to the bay. They saw nothing until the next day when they sailed around the rocky promontory where they had last seen their comrades. Rounding the tip of the promontory, to their surprise, they came upon a deep-water strait which gave every indication of running right through the encircling mountains. The supposedly lost ships suddenly appeared.

What had happened was this: the ships had been swept around the promontory by the storm and saw what appeared to be the mouth of a river. The wind and tide carried them through this narrow passage and into what seemed like a lake. Crossing the lake they traversed another narrow passage and entered a broad body of water, which discharged into several channels. Entering one of the channels they observed the marks of a forty-foot tidal drop along the steep shore. This indicated to them that this was *el paso* to the west.

The wind changed and they raced back to tell Magellan of their discovery. As the four ships continued westward the sailors continually tested the water to verify that it still kept its saltiness, thus indicating that it was part of the ocean. They also kept track of the tides so they could tell that they were going towards another ocean and not up a river.

Five weeks were consumed in getting through the Strait of Magellan as it will forever be known. Pigafetta writes, "We found by a miracle, a strait which we call the Strait of the Eleven Thousand Virgins; this strait is a hundred and ten leagues long which are four hundred and forty miles, and almost as wide as less than half a league and it issues into another sea which is called the Peaceful Sea; it is surrounded by very great and high mountains covered with snow...I think there is not in the world a more beautiful country, or a better strait than this one."

One of the ships turned and sailed for Spain, without permission, to report on the discovery of the passage into the South Sea and also to tell of the tyranny of the Captain-General and of the executions. The captain of this ship was thrown into a dungeon upon his arrival back in Spain.

On sailing into the Pacific, a solemn ceremony was held at which Magellan is said to have intoned these words, "We are about to stand into an ocean where no ship has ever sailed before. May the ocean be always as calm and benevolent as it is today. In this hope I name it the *Mar Pacifico.*"

The Pacific Ocean is rarely as calm as it was that day.

Magellan also named the cape at the western end of the Strait of Magellan Cape of Desire "as a thing which had been much desired for a long time." It is so-named today (*Cabo Deseado* in Spanish).

The Captain-General, himself, did not call the tortuous channel the Strait of Magellan, but rather Channel of All Saints (*Todos los Santos*). Some of his men are reported to have named it "Victoria vessel Strait" or "Patagones Strait."

Leaving Patagonia the three remaining ships sailed on westward until, reaching the Philippines, Magellan–the great Captain-General–was killed by some Indians. One of the ships burned, a second was lost, and the third, the *Vittoria*, returned to Spain nearly three years after embarking, with eighteen men aboard from the original 240 or so (the exact number is unclear; Pigafetta says 237 but Spanish archival records indicate more). Fortunately for history, Pigafetta was one of the eighteen. The *Vittoria* returned laden to the hatches with cloves which more than paid for the entire expedition.

A handful of the 240+ missing men eventually straggled back to Spain as they had been left at various places along the voyage. Still, the great majority were lost at sea, executed by order of their Captain-General, or killed by natives.

One of the facts reported by Pigafetta was that he had lost one day while circumnavigating the world. This was apparently puzzling to the scientists of the time. One prominent philosopher of the period explained, "That it could not have fallen out otherwise, as they had travelled for three years continuously and always accompanied the sun, which was going westward. And he told him besides, that those who sailed due westwards towards the sun, lengthen their day very much, as the ancients also had noticed."

In subsequent years a number of expeditions attempted to sail through the Strait of Magellan but most found it so difficult that they gave up. Even today it is a harrowing and difficult trip, but in the days of sailing ships it was much harder. Much of the Strait is a narrow passage, surrounded by snow-covered mountains and with very few places to land–even a small boat, let alone a sailing ship.

Drake

SIR
FRANCIS
DRAKE.

The most famous explorer of the Patagonia region after Magellan was Sir Francis Drake of England. On November 15, 1577 Drake sailed with five ships ostensibly to Alexandria in the Mediterranean. His voyage, some fifty-seven years after Magellan's, was modeled after that of the Portuguese explorer. Reportedly, he had a volume of directions from Magellan's expedition. It may well have been Pigafetta's account.

Why he pretended to be sailing to Alexandria is not clear, although given the competitiveness of explorers it may well have been done to fool other would-be round-the-world sailors.

Like Magellan, Drake stopped at the Brazilian port of St. Julian and executed a mutineer. He had the man (John Doughty) tried in front of a jury of forty and then beheaded. Doughty didn't actually lead a mutiny but was convicted only of attempting to foment one.

After Doughty's conviction and subsequent confession he was given the choice of three sentences. Either he could (1) be returned to England for retrial, (2) be marooned at Port St. Julian, or (3) be beheaded. Surprisingly, he chose to lose his head.

Before his execution, he celebrated Communion with his Captain. He then exhorted all the company to obedience, laid his head on the block of the Magellan gibbet, which was still standing after fifty-seven years, then uttered a prayer to the Queen and her realm. The ax fell and his head rolled in the sand.

Sailing to the south and past Cape Virgins, Drake entered the Strait of Magellan with his three remaining ships (he had disposed of two ships as unfit). They anchored off an island (which was probably *Isla Magdalena*, which the International Expeditions tour visits), and in one day killed 3,000 penguins. These were added to the expedition's provisions.

Sixteen days after entering the narrow channel Drake's ship *Golden Hind* (originally named *Pelican*) entered the Pacific Ocean. His was the first English ship to enter that vast ocean.

These famous lines from *The Rime of the Ancient Mariner* may refer to this event:

The fair breeze blew, the white foam flew,
The furrow followed free:
We were the first that ever burst
Into that silent sea.

After entering the Pacific, Drake turned south and may or may not have discovered Cape Horn (historians disagree on this point). One writer claims that Drake sighted an island that later disappeared into the sea as result of a volcanic eruption.

Some two hundred miles beyond the Strait and out into the Pacific he ran into a gale "the like whereof no traveller hath felt, neither hath there been such a tempest, so violent and of such continuance since Noah's flood; for it lasted full 52 days."

Regardless of what he did or did not discover, Drake then went on up the West Coast of the Americas all the way to San Francisco. Some say he even went north of there, but that is not proven.

After sailing across the Pacific and Indian Oceans and around Africa, Drake returned to England as the first Englishman to sail around the world. Drake, who many claimed was a pirate but with the English Queen's blessing, had ransacked Spanish ships and was called "the scourge of God" by the Spaniards.

Regardless of the ethics of what they did, Magellan and Drake are probably the two greatest navigators in the history of the world. It is interesting to compare the two men. Both were short, and were troubled by a sense of social inferiority. Both were experienced warriors who carried wounds from previous battles. Both were accompanied on their voyage by social superiors who felt they should have been in command. Both experienced mutinies on their circumnavigations, and each executed the mutineers in the same place.

Magellan, though discovering Tierra del Fuego, did not realize it was an island. He thought his strait was the only way from the Atlantic to the Pacific. Drake did more extensive exploration of the West Coast of Patagonia, and may, or may not, have actually discovered Cape Horn.

Drake was so hated and feared by the Spaniards that in 1579 the Spanish Viceroy in Peru dispatched a Spanish navigator, DonPedr o Sarmiento, to catch him. Sarmiento sailed for the Strait of Magellan assuming that Drake would return to England by sailing back the way he had come. Of course, Drake continued on around the world instead.

Schouten

In 1615, a very well-prepared voyage got under way from Holland. It was led by Captain

WilhelmCornelius Schouten and consisted of two ships. The smaller ship was named *Hoorn* and the larger one called, *Unity* (*Eendracht* in Dutch). They sailed from the port of Hoorn. Schouten was an extremely thorough and competent sea captain. Although sailing ships of the day normally carried a pilot among the crew, the stalwart Dutchman served as both captain and pilot.

The purpose of the expedition was not exploration but trade. Schouten and his fellow underwriter, IsaacLeMair e, intended to find a new way to the riches of the East Indies. Their intention was to open the wealth of the Moluccas to independent merchantmen in defiance of the Dutch East India Company. That quasi-governmental outfit pretty much dominated at the time what trade had been established in the Pacific, barring Dutch ships that were not part of the Dutch East India Company from sailing through the Strait of Magellan.

As was the case with earlier voyages, the goal was kept secret from the townspeople of Hoorn and other interested Dutch citizens. Schouten even went so far as to withhold that information from the crew (only the chief officers knew) until the ships were thousands of miles out to sea.

An interesting adventure on the voyage was the ramming of the *Hoorn* by a narwhal. The ship's crew was mystified by the sudden jolt they all felt. It wasn't until they reached land that they discovered what had happened. The ivory tusk of the giant narwhal had pierced three heavy planks, entering the ship by over a foot. This incident may have given Melville the idea for the episode in which the whale attacked the ship in *Moby Dick*.

Sailing south from the Strait of Magellan, the Unity (the *Hoorn* had since burned) discovered Cape Horn, named after their ship and home town. Although an island, Schouten thought it was a cape. Schouten and the *Unity* were the first Europeans and probably the first human beings to go through the channel (now called the Drake Strait) south of the land of the South American continent.

Cook

The famous English captain, James Cook, made two voyages around Cape Horn in 1769

and in 1772. Although some sixty years before Charles Darwin, Captain Cook gave a much kindlier report on the Fuegian aborigines, never mentioning the cannibalism or diabolic practices about which Darwin wrote. It is true, though, that Cook met the relatively docile Haush tribe, whereas Darwin, although he met the Haush, wrote mainly about the more aggressive Yaghan.

Cook's account is usually without the judgmental tone of Darwin. An excerpt from Cook's *Voyages of Discovery* follows: "They were of a middle stature, with broad flat faces, low foreheads, high cheeks, noses inclining to flatness, wide nostrils, small black eyes, large mouths, small but indifferent teeth, and black, straight hair falling down over their ears and forehead, which was commonly smeared with brown and red paint".

The westbound transit around Cape Horn by Captain Cook happened to be one of those rare pleasant episodes. In Cook's words, "the heavens were fair, the wind temperate, the weather pleasant".

On his second trip Cook was traveling west to east and he again found the going easy (Cook, apparently, was a lucky sailor). Landing on the island of Tierra del Fuego, but in a different part than on his earlier voyage, Cook met the Canoe Indians or the Alacaluf. His report: "They were a little ugly, half-starved, beardless race; not a tall person amongst them.... Of all the nations I have seen, these people seem to be the most wretched. They are doomed to live in one of the most inhospitable climates in the world without having sagacity enough to provide themselves with such conveniences as may render life in some measure, more comfortable." So much for Cook's nonjudgmental attitude.

East of Cape Horn Cook was driving through the cold, in constant sleet, snow, and heavy fog. He discovered the South Georgia Islands that are some 1,500 m (2,400 km) east of the Horn. Perhaps it was this voyage which prompted Coleridge to write these lines in *The Rime of the Ancient Mariner*:

> *And now there came both mist and snow,*
> *And it grew wondrous cold:*
> *And ice, mast high, came floating by,*
> *As green as emerald.*

Morris

In 1741 Isaac Morris, midshipman, and seven of his men were marooned in Patagonia. After some fifteen months, they were captured by the Indians and held for sixteen months more. Morris and his men had many adventures and suffered desperately. Morris, in his account, claims to have found many wild horses, some ridden by Indians. He writes, "The Patagonian Indians, at least those in that part of the country where we resided, are tall and well-made, being, in general, from five to six feet high, good-natured and obliging to one another and never see each other want. Tho' they have what they call a King, yet he seems to be only a Chief or Captain of the Party... They seem to have some notion of a Deity, and pay a sort of worship to the Sun and Moon."

Darwin

Although Charles Darwin was not exactly an explorer he described Patagonia in his day in great detail. As a scientist he propagated his famous theory of evolution in his best-known book, *The Origin of Species*. Darwin developed this theory following his visit to the Galapagos Islands in 1834. Darwin was a mere passenger on the English ship *Beagle*, much as Pigafetta was a passenger on Magellan's ship. However, Darwin was a scientist who recorded his research in great detail. In *The Voyage of the Beagle*, Darwin recounted the voyage that took him to the Galapagos. The Appendix on page 169 contains a lengthy excerpt from the chapter describing his visit to Patagonia.

It is surprising how accurate and insightful Darwin's observations remain today.

Additional Explorers

Subsequent English navigators who tackled the Strait of Magellan included Thomas Cavendish and John Davis. Among the early sailors, Davis experienced the wildest weather:

> *The fifth (October) our foresayle was split, and all to torne; then our Master took the mizzen, and brought it to the foremast, to make our ship work, and with our sprit-saile we mended our foresayle, the storm continuing without all reason in fury, with haile, snow, rain and wind such and so mighty, as*

*that in nature it could not possibly be
more, the seas such and so lofty, with
continual breach, that many times we
were doubtful whether our ship did sink
or swim.*

In 1598 the first Dutch ship navigated the Strait of Magellan.

Neither those early Dutchmen nor any of the others who transited the Strait of Magellan during those years knew, or even suspected, that there was another way to go from the Atlantic to the Pacific. That way was around Cape Horn, far to the south.

A generation later CaptainJohn Narbor ough, an Englishman, was commissioned to sail around South America on a voyage of observation.

One of the following sailors who 'rounded the Horn' had some bad luck and subsequently shot an albatross, since there was a superstition of the sea that an albatross brought bad luck. This event was apparently the basis for the section in Coleridge's *The Rime of the Ancient Mariner* that reads as follows:

[The Ancient Mariner addresses the Wed-
ding Guest]
*At length did cross an Albatross,
Through the fog it came;
As if it had been a Christian soul,
We hailed it in God's name.*

It ate the food it ne'er had eat,
And round and round it flew.
The ice did split with a thunder-fit;
The helmsman steered us through!

And a good south wind sprung up behind;
The Albatross did follow,
And every day, for food or play,
Came to the mariner's hollo!

In mist or cloud, on mast or shroud,
It perched for vespers nine;
Whiles all the night, through fog-smoke white,
Glimmered the white Moon-shine.

[The Wedding Guest asks:]

God save thee, ancient Mariner!
From the fiends, that plague thee thus!—
Why look'st thou so?—

* * *

With my cross-bow
I shot the albatross.

The poet, Samuel Coleridge, had read the
account of the first sailors to round Cape Horn,
and incorporated many of their adventures into
his poem.

One of the first disasters while rounding the Horn was, ironically, not a result of the terrible weather, but rather the result of fire. A French frigate, *Le Prince*, was sailing eastward of the Horn in the South Atlantic when it was found to be afire. The ship burned and then blew up. Only ten men survived out of 300. The ten, in a small boat, managed to make their way some 600 miles to southern Brazil.

As the ship was burning and most of the crew had jumped overboard, nine men were clinging to a spar that was floating in the water. Unfortunately, one of the cannons had been left loaded. When the fire reached the gunpowder, the gun fired and the ball hit the floating spar, killing several of the men and wounding the rest.

In 1767 the first woman circumnavigated the world, sailing through the Strait of Magellan in the process. She was a Frenchwoman masquerading as a man and assuming the duties of a servant.

It is interesting to note that serving on board James Cook's ship was a young man in his early twenties by the name of William Bligh. This was the notorious Captain Bligh of *The Mutiny on the Bounty.*

Some fifteen years after serving with Cook, Bligh was captain of his own ship and attempted to round the Horn. He couldn't do it. He spent twenty-nine days trying, but *Bounty's* log records a succession of tempests, with rain, sleet, hail, and snow. The current, the wind, and the series of storms made it impossible, and he finally turned and ran for Africa's Cape of Good Hope. The miserable conditions on board during this struggle gave an indication of the stubbornness of Bligh and makes the later mutiny somewhat understandable.

CaptainDavid Porter, US Navy, doubled Cape Horn in 1813 during the War of 1812. He also was lucky enough to encounter relatively moderate wind and storms while sailing from the Atlantic to the Pacific. Even so, he wrote these words of warning to subsequent sea captains: "The passage round Cape Horn, from the eastward, I assert, from my own experience is the most dangerous, most difficult, and attended with more hardships, than that of the same distance, in any other part of the world; and none should attempt it, without using every precaution to guard against accident, that prudence or foresight can suggest."

Porter then proceeded to give specific instructions re what sails to use, exactly where to sail, etc. He ended with this advice, "I would advise those bound into the Pacific, never to attempt the passage of Cape Horn, if they can get there by any other route."

In 1826 began the most thorough exploration and charting of the Tierra del Fuego area than had yet been done. A British expedition was led by CaptainParker King in the *Adventure* with

CaptainRobert FitzRoy commanding the *Beagle*. This was a scientific expedition a great deal more sophisticated than any that had ever been attempted before here at the bottom of the world. Their scientific instruments included dip circles and magnetic cylinders for magnetic observations, accurate chronometers, sextants, and station pointers to name but a few of the new devices available. Their findings filled several volumes. Charting the many creeks and inlets, identifying the innumerable channels, islets, and glaciers, they also named the thousands of islands. They measured the currents that surged throughout as well as the rivers, waterfalls, and glaciers. The expedition arrived at the heights of the mountains and the tides, tested the soil and the rocks, cataloged the trees, plants, and mosses, sketched the animals and birds, and discovered new breeds.

Although this most comprehensive survey is still the basis for what is known about the southern part of Patagonia, it is not the final word. Even today there are still unexplored areas and unnamed geographical features. At least one bay (Condor Bay) visited nowadays by the *Terra Australis* has been named by the crew of the ship. The naming of features, at least on the Chilean side, is the responsibility of the Chilean Navy. The Captain of the *Terra Australis* told me that the application is pending.

It would seem that the greedy European merchants would have sent ship after ship around

South America once two routes had been discovered. After all, the riches of the East were there, it was thought at the time, for exploitation. Also, the vast amounts of gold that had been uncovered along the West Coast of South America, particularly in Mexico and Peru, needed to be shipped back home to Spain. But there were only a few brave souls who risked the perilous voyage through the Magellan and Drake Straits.

There had already been too many shipwrecks on these dangerous routes. Thus the merchants of the time sent ships around the Cape of Good Hope in Africa. The Spanish treasure ships that were decimating Peru sailed up the West Coast of South America and then transported their gold and silver across the Isthmus of Panama by a difficult (and also dangerous) land bridge to the Atlantic, still thought of as less dangerous than the Magellan or Drake Straits.

Actually the Dutch did send two large expeditions around South America and into the Pacific in efforts to destroy Spanish power in South America. These two expeditions, one in 1624 and the other in 1643, both failed, but surprisingly not because of the weather. Both had reasonably favorable weather conditions around the Horn but both captains grew ill and died and the expeditions deteriorated and failed to achieve their goal. After these two disastrous failures the Dutch quit trying to invade the Pacific.

From the time of Pythagoras, some five centuries before the birth of Christ, the ancients believed in the existence of Antichthon or an "Anti-Earth" in the far south. This supposedly was an upside-down country where snow fell upward, trees grew downwards, the sun shone black, and its inhabitants were the sixteen-fingered Antipodeans. It was believed to be a sort of Hell. Dante who described it in his *Inferno* shared this belief. Dante's description was used by Tennyson in his poem *Ulysses*, by Poe in his *The Narrative of Arthur Gordon Pym*, and by Melville in *Moby Dick*.

Superstition still exists in the world today but it does not dictate human behavior nearly as much as it did in the seventeenth century. There was not only a great deal of fear of the terrible physical conditions that existed in Patagonia but also a fear of the "unseen forces" that were believed to exist there.

EARLY DEVELOPMENTS

Giants

Magellan's chronicler, Antonio Pigafetta, writes:

> But one day, (without anyone expecting it) we saw a giant who was on the shore, quite naked, and who danced, leaped, and sang, and while he sang he threw sand and dust on his head. Our captain sent one of our men toward him, charging him to leap and

> *sing like the other in order to reassure him and to show him friendship. Which he did. And when he was before us, he began to marvel and to be afraid, and he raised one finger upward, believing that we came from heaven. And he was so tall that the tallest of us only came up to his waist.*

Thus began one of the strangest beliefs in history. Many other chroniclers for several centuries claimed to have seen these giants.

In 1615, Admiral Spilbergen, leader of a Dutch expedition, reported seeing "a Man of gigantic Stature climbing the hills, to take a view of them." He evidently saw a Tehuelche Indian.

This fit into the belief at the time that the people who lived near the poles of the earth were taller. (I guess this belief had something to do with gravity)! The truth is that there were no giants–only large, tall muscular men with elaborate hairdos that made them seem even taller.

Among other observations made by Captain Narborough in the 17th century, he measured the Patagonians who lived around Cape Desire. He found the tallest to be 5 ft and 11 $1/2$ in (182 cm). This discredited the stories of gigantic natives. Pigafetta and the others who claimed to have seen giants were then deemed liars. Nevertheless, the Indians measured by Narborough were probably of the Alacaluf tribe, whereas Magellan had presumably visited the taller Tehuelche.

Darwin writes:

> *"During our previous visit (in January), we had an interview at Cape Gregory with the famous so-called gigantic Patagonians, who gave us a cordial reception. Their height appears greater than it really is, from their large guanaco mantles, their long flowing hair, and general figure: on an average, their height is about six feet, with some men taller and only a few shorter; and the women are also tall; altogether they are certainly the tallest race which we anywhere saw."*

As Bourne writes in his 1853 book, *The Captive in Patagonia: Life Among the Giants*, "As we approached the beach, a crowd of black-looking giants came to the water's edge to gaze at us." He later describes these giants as being about a head taller than he was (5'10") with an average height of 6 $1/2$ ft (2 m) with some people nearly 7 ft (213 cm) tall.

Allen Gardiner

The story of Allen Gardiner's foray into early-day Patagonia is a tragic one. Captain Allen Gardiner of the Royal Navy was born in 1794. He had traveled to distant parts of the British Empire and was considered to be tough. In 1834, he lost his wife, retired from the Navy, and dedicated himself to bringing the Gospel to the heathen. He was a man of strong faith but, apparently, little common sense. Trying to find a place for his missionary work, he looked first at Zululand, then New Guinea. He investigated Bolivia, but finally settled on Patagonia, particularly Tierra del Fuego.

Gardiner founded the Patagonia Missionary Society and, in 1848, sailed from England for Lima, Peru. He had four sailors accompanying him, and the coal ship had agreed to put his party ashore on Tierra del Fuego with their whale-boat, their dinghy, and six months' rations. Although the party was put ashore Gardiner quickly saw that it was not a feasible plan. It was the beginning of winter, the natives were certain to be hostile, and a storm of such fury was raging that the landing party couldn't even pitch their tents. So the five men immediately decided to get back on the ship and return to England.

Soon after, in 1850, Gardiner hitched another ride from England for Tierra del Fuego, this time with two 24-foot metal boats, each with its own dinghy, and seven men as the crew. The ship that carried them deposited them, as before, on Picton Island south of Tierra del Fuego. The ship's last sight of the eight men found them standing on the deck of their boats singing hymns.

Upon looking over their supplies they discovered that they had neglected to bring their reserve supply of ammunition. This was a devastating blow, as without ammunition they could neither feed themselves nor protect themselves from the hostile natives. Soon, natives harassed them and took from the whites whatever they wished. More and more natives surrounded them and grew increasingly unpleasant. Finally the whites fled to their boats and pulled them offshore. The natives loaded their canoes with large stones, which they were experts at throwing. Gardiner and his group rowed away, but they couldn't row their boats fast enough, so the natives in their light canoes soon caught up with the would-be missionaries. Just when it seemed that the interlopers were going to be caught and killed, a strong breeze sprang up, the metal boats quickly hoisted sail and fled from the frustrated natives.

The escapees, looking for a place to hide, found a secluded cove some fifteen miles from where they had first landed. However, the natives eventually found them and the group had to put to sea again. They were forced to run from the people they had come to save. During their flight a gale struck, and they lost both their dinghies; their provisions were seriously damaged by sea water.

Finally they managed to paint on a rock at the entrance of a cove instructions as to where they could be found. Also Gardiner left some letters and a message in a bottle. The message urged the rescue party to hurry up (I said Gardiner was a dreamer). The eight men barely survived a very severe winter. One of their boats washed ashore and was damaged beyond repair. They got scurvy. Some provisions they had hidden in a cave were ruined by an unusually high tide resulting from a violent storm. They ran out of food and survived on a fox they had trapped, a few fish and sea-birds that were washed ashore, shellfish, and seaweed.

One by one the men died. Gardiner was the last to expire, leaving written instructions as to how the missionary work was to continue. These instructions were followed, with Gardiner's successor bringing his family with him to the Falkland Islands, and eventually to Tierra del Fuego. His family included an adopted 13-year-old boy named Thomas Bridges. This boy was destined to become the domineering figure in Patagonia for the next several decades.

Thomas Bridges

Gardiner's fiasco took place in 1851, but by 1859 it was deemed safe to retry establishing a mission on, or near, Tierra del Fuego. Several of the natives had spent some time in the Falkland Islands with Gardiner's group and had learned some English. Also, Thomas Bridges had been particularly proficient at learning the Yaghan language. Surprisingly, and probably fortunately, he was not included in the next effort to establish a mission among the Patagonian Indians.

That effort ended in a massacre. Although somewhat harassed by the natives, the missionaries proceeded to build a small church anyway and to hold a church service in it. However, the Indians were enraged because they had been accused of theft, particularly those who had been in the Falkland Islands staying with the missionaries. Upon searching their possessions as they departed the Falklands the theft (of tools, biscuits, and other odds and ends) was validated, and this enraged the Indians even more. Thus, the first church service in Patagonia culminated in the slaughter of the whites by the Indians. Only the cook survived, as he had stayed on board the ship rather than attend the church service. The cook fled into the wilderness but eventually was captured and lived for three months with the Indians before being returned to civilization.

The theft of minor household items by the Indians was certainly truly stealing and wrong in the eyes of the Englishmen. But was it wrong in the eyes of the natives? Their lifestyle appeared to call for the sharing of all possessions. The culture of the native Patagonians was very different from that of Europe. An example of the cultural gap can be seen in the complaints of Darwin during his visit to Patagonia. Writing of the (probably Yaghan) Indians, he says:

*Young and old, men and children,
never ceased repeating the word
"yammerschooner," which means
"give me." After pointing to almost
every object, one after the other, even
to the buttons on our coats, and saying their favourite word in as many
intonations as possible, they would
then use it in a neuter sense, and va-
cantly repeat "yammerschooner."*

*After yammerschoonering for any ar-
ticle very eagerly, they would by a
simple artifice point to their young
women or little children, as much as
to say, "If you will not give it me,
surely you will to such as these."*

The Indians had many social customs that
were strictly observed; although lying and stealing were common, calling a man a liar or thief
was a serious insult. Failure to recognize this fact
cost at least seven lives. Who is to say that the
Christian view of morality is the only one?

Following the massacre and the rescue of the
cook, the Indians, probably from fear of reprisal,
became friendly and cooperative. But the remaining missionaries, after rejecting the idea of re-
venge, decided not to pursue the establishment
of a mission on Tierra del Fuego. They returned
to England.

However, they did leave the eighteen-year-old Thomas Bridges ashore on the Falkland Islands with a few Yaghan. Bridges remained at his own request and, with the help of the Yaghans, proceeded to learn the language of the Indians. It is a very intricate and, in some ways, sophisticated language that was difficult for an Englishman to acquire. Yet Bridges began to compile a dictionary of the Yaghan language, a lifelong undertaking that culminated in the publication of the only Yaghan-English dictionary. But the dictionary was by no means Bridges' only accomplishment.

Bridges' first arrival in Tierra del Fuego had been in 1863, when he accompanied the new chief missionary sent from England. The young man served chiefly as an interpreter. For the next several years Bridges visited the Indians regularly and brought more than fifty friends to stay in the Falklands. Finally, late in 1867, a settlement was successfully established on Navarin Island, south of Tierra del Fuego and across the Beagle Channel. This was the fourth time that the establishment of a settlement had been attempted.

This fourth effort was different in that it was primarily a settlement of natives learning to be farmers. Later, a settlement partly of whites was established on Tierra del Fuego at Ushuaia. In 1868 the English missionary society ordered Bridges back to England to take Holy Orders. He returned to Tierra del Fuego in 1870 and for fifteen years was in charge of the Ushuaia mission. He kept a diary, and his son Lucas published a book compiled from the diaries and other sources called **Uttermost Part of the Earth**. The adventures and experiences of both father and son make for a very interesting and enjoyable read.

Jemmy Button

Sometimes referred to as Jimmy, Jemmy Button was actually a Yaghan Indian. On May 11, 1830, as a teenager, he was in a canoe with some men of his clan as they approached an English ship that was exploring in the area. The only account we have of what next occurred is what is written in the journal of CaptainRobert FitzRoy, the commander of the Beagle who was in charge of the whaleboat that day:

> "...we continued our route, but were stopped when in sight of the Narrows by three canoes full of natives, anxious for barter. We gave them a few beads and buttons, for some fish; and, without any previous intention, I told one of the boys in a canoe to come into our boat, and gave the man who was with him a large shining mother-of-pearl button. The boy got into my boat directly, and sat down. Seeing him and his friends seem quite contented, I

*pulled onwards, and, a light breeze
springing up made sail. Thinking that
this accidental occurrence might prove
useful to the natives, as well as to ourselves, I determined to take advantage
of it. The canoe, from which the boy
came, paddled towards the shore...* "

The boy's name in his native tongue had been
Orundellico but he was now named Jemmy Button. FitzRoy's version of what transpired may
not be quite accurate. The Captain was known
to be a bigoted man who believed in the neces-
sity of slavery. It could well be that he falsified
the story to justify abduction. We will never
know.

FitzRoy had had a great deal of trouble with
the native Fuegians, since they were prone to
thievery. In the course of the same voyage, he
took three other natives. Again, whether they
were hostages or guests is unclear. The three were
named: Fuegia Basket, a pleasant but exceedingly
fat young girl of about eight; York Minister, a
sullen brute, who later became quite enamored
of Fuegia Basket and eventually took her as his
wife; and Boat Memory, who was apparently
captured and made prisoner.

The four were taken back to England where
they were "educated" in English and Christian
ways. Although Jemmy Button was a Yaghan, the
other three were Alacaluf. FitzRoy reportedly
took good care of his charges, and had them

vaccinated, a new procedure that had only recently become common. In spite of this, Boat Memory died of smallpox shortly after reaching England. The others stayed with various families, learning English as well as manners and general deportment. They were even introduced to the king and queen!

Of the three remaining Fuegians, York Minister was an uncooperative and not very communicative individual. Fuegia Basket was charming and a quick learner but still a child. Jemmy Button, on the other hand, was a handsome young man who was eager to please. He was also quite vain. He preened himself before every mirror he passed. He loved to wear fancy clothes with shining shoes and kid gloves.

After fourteen months in England the three were returned to Tierra del Fuego. They were again passengers on the *Beagle*, captained by FitzRoy. Charles Darwin was also a passenger on this particular voyage.

It is Jemmy Button's story we can follow as nothing much of note was recorded concerning the other two, other than that they eventually married. Jemmy, once back in Patagonia, quickly reverted to his pre-English ways. Some thirteen months after being returned to his people, Jemmy was found nearly naked, emaciated, and with long dirty hair. As Darwin writes, "It was quite painful to behold him…. When he left us he was very fat, and so particular about his clothes, that he was always afraid of even dirtying his shoes;

scarcely ever without gloves and his hair neatly cut. I never saw so complete and grievous a change."

Jemmy was quite content and refused the offer of returning to England. This surprised Darwin, FitzRoy, and their colleagues aboard the English ship. Jemmy certainly looked miserable (to the Englishmen) but actually he was quite content. Around this time he was the victim of extensive thievery by York Minister and some other Alacaluf. Despite this he chose to return to his people. This was in 1834.

Twenty-one years later–in 1855–Jemmy Button was again seen by Europeans, this time by an expedition of the Patagonia Missionary Society led by CaptainW illiam Snow. By this time he had two wives, several children, and had gained a great deal of weight. He, of course, was still in his preferred disheveled state, but he quickly resumed speaking English and reverted to his English-taught manners. Nevertheless he refused to return with Captain Snow to the Falklands. He showed some hostility towards the members of the Snow expedition.

Finally, after another visit to Tierra del Fuego in 1858, the missionaries prevailed upon Jemmy and several members of his family to come over to the Falkland Islands for a period of time. After several months, the Button family was returned to their homeland while nine other Fuegians were recruited.

A few days after they got back to their settlement the previously described massacre of 1859 took place. There is strong reason to believe that Jemmy Button was one of the leaders of the massacre!

After many generations, I hope we've learned that if we get away from the judging of another culture by the standards of our own we can see more clearly the value of every culture.

IV

NATIVE GROUPS

Perhaps as early as 30,000 years ago people had crossed into North America from Siberia. Evidence has been found that indigenous people lived in the southern Lake District of Chile some 13,000 years ago. The Lake District of Chile is north of what we consider Patagonia. It is believed that humans arrived in Tierra del Fuego about 8,000 years ago. This migration, all the way through the Americas from Siberia to Tierra del Fuego, took several thousand years and may have constituted the longest migration in human history.

The indigenous people of Patagonia separated into several groups. The word tribe does not apply as this word implies the existence of a leader or chief. From what is known about the indigenous people of Patagonia it seems they did not have leaders. A note: the word Indian, although inaccurate, is used at various places in this book to describe the native peoples only because it is a familiar term and is used in much of the literature on Patagonia.

The northernmost group was known as Mapuche. They were divided into sub-groups; three of them being the Puelche, the Pehuenche, and the Huilliche. The three had very different lifestyles, particularly in their forms of sustenance. For instance, the Pehuenche people survived largely on the fruit of the araucaria tree while the Huilliche, living along the West Coast, were less nomadic and practiced slash-and-burn agriculture. This was probably the only group of native people in Patagonia who relied primarily on farming.

South of the Mapuche, and more important for our purposes, lived the Tehuelche. They were quite tall and nomadic hunters. They hunted primarily guanaco and occupied the steppes in the eastern part of Patagonia from about the Río Negro in Argentina south to the Strait of Magellan. The southernmost group of the Tehuelche were known as Aónikenk.

Tehuelche

As mentioned earlier the Tehuelches were the so-called Patagonian giants. Apparently, the natives had guanaco wool twisted into their hair in such a way that it made them look much taller than they really were. That, along with their muscular physique, made them appear to be giants. They were wiped out in the nineteenth century primarily by disease. Also, many Tehuelches were killed by European and Argentine settlers. Photos actually exist of Tehuelches being hunted and killed by whites.

The Tehuelches apparently were opposed to beards; even though they had hairy faces, they pulled out these facial hairs. Or, rather, had their women pull them out. Reportedly, they never washed their hair. According to one writer, they were extremely lazy, except when they were hunting. Tehuelches hunted primarily guanacos, the skins of which had many uses. For instance, their dwellings were constructed of wooden poles covered with guanaco skins. They disdained fishing. Although some writers believed that the Tehuelches had no religion or organization, others claimed that they had chiefs. They had no sense of the past or the future. Nor did they have any rituals or ceremonies. They did not believe in a god but they did fear an evil spirit they called Wolische. Their skin coloration was described as bronze with just a touch of red.

Different writers saw and described various customs of the Tehuelche and the other Indians.

This is because the tribes ranged over a large area and so many different customs evolved. Also, of course, visitors wrote at different periods from 1519 to 1985. During these years practices of the native peoples changed. For instance, the hunting techniques of the Tehuelche changed significantly with the introduction of the horse and the gun.

South of the Strait of Magellan there were four distinct groups of Indians. Collectively they are sometimes called Fuegians or Firelanders, but individually they are Ona, Haush, Alacaluf, and Yaghan.

The northern part of Tierra del Fuego was occupied by the Ona people. Like the Tehuelche, the Ona were primarily hunters. The Ona (or Selk'nam) were similar to the Tehuelches both linguistically and in their hunting way of life. Another, but smaller, group was called the Haush (or Mannenkenk) who lived in the southeastern section of the island. There is some reason to believe that the Ona and the Haush were enemies who occasionally fought each other.

It was the Ona fires on the south shore of the Strait of Magellan that led Magellan to name the island Tierra del Fuego (Land of Fire). Their language was said to be so similar to that of the Tehuelches that individuals from the two groups could easily understand each other. The Ona, like the Tehuelche, were fierce and aggressive. They were the feared aristocrats of Tierra del Fuego

Island as the Tehuelches were of the area north of the Strait of Magellan. The Ona also were large, the men averaging about six feet with muscular arms and legs.

Lucas Bridges, in his book *Uttermost Part of the Earth*, says of the Ona, "They were as different from the Yaghan and Alacaloof (sic) as Redskins from Ancient Britons." Bridges should know as he was born in Ushuaia in 1874 and grew up helping his missionary father. He learned and recorded a great deal about the various Indians and about Tierra del Fuego. He became so close to the Ona that he was initiated into their secrets.

Ona speech was guttural, harsh, and short. They were amazingly quick, both in sight and movement. Bridges describes a ritual ceremony where an Ona man starts running, from about ninety yards, towards a bowman who quickly shoots five arrows in rapid succession directly at the running target. The targeted man successfully dodged the arrows. For the purpose of this ceremony the arrowheads were replaced with pieces of hide which prevented any wounds from being mortal. In the few instances when the arrows struck the man, it resulted in only bleeding wounds, which were completely ignored by the bleeder.

In his book, Bridges recounts a number of Ona legends. They evidently were a very imaginative people. The Ona had no religion but did believe in the existence of evil spirits. Or, rather, they pretended to in order to scare their women. One of their legends held that, in ancient times, the women of the tribe were dominant and the men lived in fear and subjection. At that time the women had their own lodge which men were not allowed to enter. The females had powers of witchcraft that could cause illness and death. The tyranny of the women grew worse and worse until the men revolted and killed all the adult women. In order to prevent the resurgence of the domination of women as the remaining young girls grew into women, the men eventually created their own lodge to which women were not allowed, under penalty of death, to enter. This lodge, called a *hain*, existed well into the twentieth century.

The main prey of the Ona was the guanaco, although they hunted deer and rhea as well. They were skilled trackers. In addition to the meat from hunted animals they also ate roots, wild celery, and berries. It is known that they lived by hunting, using both bows and arrows and the bola. Working only with crude tools, the Ona managed to make bows and arrows of superb craftmanship.

The *bola* (which means ball) is a weapon made of two or three 2 in (5 cm) balls of iron or stone. A stout cord, about 3 ft (1 m) long, is fastened to each ball. Then the cords are tied together in a large knot. Hunting is done by grasping the knot, twirling the balls around one's head, and then releasing them in the direction of the prey. If well thrown the balls cause the cords to wrap around the legs of the guanaco or other animal and bring it down. The bola is thrown somewhat like a lasso or boomerang. Souvenir replicas may be purchased in Ushuaia. It became a hunting weapon of the Argentine gaucho or cowboy. It may still be in use in the Argentine pampas.

The customs of the Ona were similar to those of the Aónikenk. They adapted well to the harsh climate of Tierra del Fuego. There are indications that they traded with the Yaghan, meeting them in the mountain passes near present-day Ushuaia. Following the introduction of sheep ranching the Ona began to kill the sheep, since it was certainly easier to hunt docile sheep than to stalk the elusive guanacos. Not surprisingly, this enraged the ranchers and they began hunting the Indians. It is reported that at one time professional killers received a bounty for each pair of Ona ears they obtained.

Estimates indicate that in 1880 the Ona population reached 4,000 individuals; however, by 1919 the population had shrunk to barely 279 individuals (mixed individuals or mestizos are not counted); and in 1931 their population dropped to eighty-four individuals who were found to be in poor health. In 1964 only forty Ona were counted; on December 8, 1994, with the death of Paachek, the last pure Ona, this ethnic group became extinct.

Ona family

Museum Saliesano

A much different group of native Patagonians were known as the Canoe Indians. They lived along the waterways of the western and southern islands of Patagonia. The Canoe Indians can be divided into two broad groups. Around the Beagle Channel and the southern islands were the Yaghan (or Yamana) while the Alacaluf (also known as Kawéskar or Halakwulup) lived among the western islands.

Early explorers viewed the Yaghan as extremely primitive, partly because they wore very few clothes. This was a puzzle to the Europeans, particularly in view of the harsh climate. However, the Yaghan apparently greased themselves with whale or seal oil to insulate from the cold. Also, somehow they had become adapted to the climate over the centuries. Covering themselves with grease made them quite comfortable in temperatures that were still very uncomfortable for the white visitors, even with their layers of clothing.

Yaghans often lived in places where there were no beaches for their canoes. Thus the women (who were the canoe paddlers), after unloading the canoe and their men, would paddle out to a kelp bed and secure their canoe to the seaweed. Once the canoe was anchored in this fashion the woman would slip into the freezing water and swim ashore.

Thomas Bridges once measured some thirty Yaghan men. Their height varied from 5 ft, 5 in (1.6 m) to 4 ft, 8 in (1.4 m). Although short they were very strong. Yaghan men and women sometimes wore a tiny apron made of otter-skin and had a second garment of the same material, which they either wore over their shoulders or tied to their bodies.

The Yaghan greasing themselves is not unlike what long-distance swimmers do in our modern world. Swimmers stroking across the English Channel, for instance, cover themselves with grease to keep out the cold.

Unfortunately the Europeans saw only dirty, greasy savages. But these "savages" had designed and built canoes that were ideally shaped for the waters in the area. Modern naval architects could not do better.

Perhaps it is only fair to compare some of their accomplishments with that of other native peoples. Take the axe, for instance, which to Native Americans (before the introduction of iron) was a heavy, blunt object enabling its wielder to crush the skill of an enemy. The Yaghan's axe was a relatively delicate instrument with its head made of shell. Thus it had a keen edge and was ideal for its purpose, which was primarily to cut down trees for use in making canoes, harpoons, and other useful items.

Another comparison can be made in the area of language. An early Eskimo-English dictionary had fewer than 2,500 words. Even Shakespeare had a vocabulary of only 24,000 words; but the Yaghan language contained upwards of 40,000 words!

An unusual aspect of the Yaghan culture is the fact that they carried burning fires in their canoes. A Yaghan canoe had a 2 or 3 sq ft (.2 to .3 sq m) section of inverted sod as the base for the fire. Before the coming of the white man the Yaghan were a nomadic people and the idea of carrying their fire with them made a lot of sense.

A Yaghan canoe can be seen in the museum at Punta Arenas. Their marital customs were interesting. The Yaghan were monogamous and actually refused to allow their members to be single. Men and women had equal rights and they believed in divorce.

A Yaghan child passed from childhood to adulthood by going through an initiation ceremony called *ciexaus*. Ciexaus went on for ten days, during which the boy or girl remained hungry, cold, and blindfolded. The ceremony ended with singing, dancing, and games.

Some authorities believe that none of the Patagonian Indians had religious beliefs, but other writers say that the Yaghan believed in a superior being named Watawuinewua.

The white man, particularly the seal and whale hunters, brought with them diseases and introduced alcohol. The combination led to the extinction of this ethnic group.

Thomas Bridges, the missionary who lived among the Yaghan, studied their ways and words. He found them to be a bright and quick-witted people. The Yaghan were also known as the Yamana (the people). The name Yaghan actually came into use when Thomas Bridges shortened the term Yahgashagalumoala to Yaghan. Yahgashagalumoala referred only to the inhabitants of what is today Murray Narrows, but Yaghan became the popular name for the entire tribe.

Charles Darwin, while a naturalist on FitzRoy's *Beagle,* had this to say about the Indians (Yaghans) he encountered: "the most abject and miserable creatures I anywhere beheld.... Viewing such men, one can hardly make oneself believe that they are fellow creatures, and inhabitants of the same world." This judgmental comment was unlike Darwin's usual scientific objectivity. Perhaps he was suffering a touch of sea-sickness?

Compared to the English and other settlers all the native groups did seem extremely primitive. But they had rich oral traditions and their vocabulary matched or exceeded that of other cultures. Although living in a harsh and uncompromising land and climate, their tools, weapons, and their very bodies were adapted for survival.

The Alacaluf were nomads who traveled, mostly by canoe, through islands and channels in the western part of the archipelago. They lived primarily by fishing but they also harvested mussels and hunted seals and sea lions. The climate in their territory was very harsh, with heavy rainfall, hurricane-force winds, and freezing water.

They lived in small, isolated groups. Their canoes were made of three pieces of bark tied together by vegetable fiber or whale whiskers, and caulked with a mixture of clay and roots. They also made dugout canoes. On land they lived in tents made of sticks and covered with the skins of sea lions. The Alacaluf sometimes wore a piece of sealskin that covered their back and chest. At other times they simply covered their naked bodies with animal oil mixed with earth to protect themselves from the harsh climate. This, of course, was what led the English to call them "naked miserable savages." Fashionwise they wore feathers on their arms and a kind of feather tiara on their foreheads. They wore necklaces of shell or beads of polished bone. For additional decoration they painted their bodies with red, white, and black lines.

According to contemporary accounts the Alacaluf were short with stocky torsos and arms, but their legs were skinny and weak, apparently as a result of their adaptation to life on the water. Their skin was a coppery color. As they covered themselves with seal lard they smelled strongly. Like the Yaghan, while sailing they kept a fire lit in the middle of their boats. This was for cooking food and also kept their young children warm. Men and women had clearly defined duties: the men made the canoes, tents, weapons, and tools for fishing and hunting, while women made handicrafts and nets, prepared the skins and extracted seafood, and took care of the cooking. Only the women knew how to swim, and they were in charge of looking after the children, maneuvering the canoe, and keeping the fire lit.

The Alacaluf's weapons consisted of spears, serrated harpoons made of whalebone and wood, bolas, and stones.

They apparently had no belief in a higher power, but they did believe in evil spirits. It was taboo to eat raw mussels. The shells were not to be thrown into the sea. Dogs were kept but were not eaten because they believed that eating dogs caused storms. A person's death brought bad weather, illness, unfruitful hunting, physical handicaps, and fear. An initiation ceremony for young people was held in which masks were worn. The participants suffered in various ways and were deprived of things. The ceremony instilled discipline that was considered essential for adulthood.

The Yaghan and the Alacaluf understood each other's language much like the Tehuelche and the Ona could communicate with each other. This may or may not indicate that the Yaghan and the Alacaluf were originally of one blood line and the Tehuelche and the Ona another. The Yaghan and the Alacaluf occasionally inter-married.

The Indians must have been thoroughly confused by the many ways the early white visitors to their land treated them. Some of the explorers attempted to get along with the natives, but then later took some as captives. Others, whether Spanish, Dutch, French, or English, simply shot them when they began stealing. Theft was, apparently, an accepted part of their culture but the whites were explorers, not anthropologists. A few of the early visitors, like Cook, attempted to understand the locals rather than simply judge them.

There were instances of cooperation between the natives and the interlopers. For instance, the Tehuelche, who had been treated very badly by earlier Spaniards, and who were a fierce, proud people, spent months helping a shipwrecked Spanish crew build a new ship in the 1760s.

Deep down, neither the Indians nor the Europeans seemed to have hostile intentions, but the clash of cultural expectations plus language problems led to misunderstandings on both sides. An example occurred in 1690 when the crew of an English man-of-war anchored in the strait and began fishing:

> *These natives (Alakalufs[sic])*
> *were amicable with us till our people*
> *went to fish where some of them were.*
> *They had also some small nets with*
> *which they supplied and contented*
> *themselves, till unfortunately they saw*
> *our people fishing with our seine which*
> *was 80 fathoms long. Then great num-*
> *ber of fishes we caught raised first their*
> *amazement, and then their indigna-*
> *tion, which increased to that height*
> *that they began to give our men dis-*
> *turbance by pelting them with clods.*
> *The English fishermen replied with*
> *musket fire "by which some of the na-*
> *tives were wounded."*

This familiar confrontation is still going on today–between small fishermen who make their living from the sea and the large corporations who harvest huge numbers of fish from the same waters.

Just as the Europeans were confused and appalled by the practices and lifestyles of the Indians, so the invaders' ways puzzled the natives.

The idea that sharing of property was considered a crime could only have been perplexing to the locals. In addition, the Europeans' obvious love of ceremonies was probably met with amusement. Whether raising or lowering flags, firing off signal cannons, or erecting crosses and kneeling before them, these bearded white people did some very odd things. These native people lived from day to day, and had few rituals and beliefs (at least as far as the Europeans could discover).

The first (and erroneous) report of cannibalism by the Indians was written in 1624: "They more resemble beasts than men...they tear men to pieces, and devour the flesh raw and bloody." Darwin believed this report and elaborated upon it with the help of a little Yaghan boy who told the scientist that in winter his tribe smoked to death their old women by holding them over a fire before eating the tastier portions. The child even imitated the screams of the women. Later research by other scientists disproved the man-eating allegations. It is established that cannibalism was never practiced by any of the Patagonian Indians. Bet that kid must have had a good time fooling the great (and gullible) scientist!

In 1769, Cook writes of the Indians (probably the Haush) he encountered:

> *They are something above the middle size, of a dark copper color with long black hair; they paint their bodies*

in streaks, mostly red and black. Their clothing consists wholly in a guanaco skin or that of a seal, in the same form as it came from the animal's back. The women wear a piece of skin over their privy parts, but the men observe no such decency. Their huts are made like a beehive, and open on one side where they have their fires; they are made of small sticks and covered with branches of trees, long grass, etc., in such a manner that they are neither proof against wind, hail, rain or snow, a sufficient proof that these people must be a very hardy race. They live chiefly on shell fish, such as mussels, which they gather from off the rocks along the sea-shore, and this seems to be the work of the women. Their arms are bows and arrows neatly made; their arrows are bearded, some with glass and others with fine flint; several pieces of the former we saw amongst them with other European things, such as rings, buttons, cloth, canvas, etc., which I think proves that they must sometimes travel to the northward, as we know of no ship that hath been in these parts for many years; besides, they were not at all surprised at our firearms; on the contrary, they seemed to know the use

*of them, by making signs to us to fire
at seals or birds that might come in the
way. They have no boats that we saw
or anything to go upon the water with;
their number doth not exceed fifty or
sixty young and old, and there are
fewer women than men. They are extremely fond of any red thing, and
seemed to set more value on beads than
anything we could give them; in this
consists their whole pride, few, either
men or women, are without a necklace
or string of beads made of small shells
or bones about their necks. They would
not taste any strong liquor, neither did
they seem fond of our provisions. We
could not discover that they had any
head or chief or any form of government, neither have they any useful or
necessary utensil except it be a bag or
basket to gather their mussels into. In
a word they are perhaps as miserable
set of people as are this day upon earth.*

Magellan's interaction with the Indians of
Patagonia (probably Tehuelche) is reported by
Pigafetta:

*One day we suddenly saw a naked
man of giant stature on the shores of
the port, dancing, singing, and throw-*

ing dust on his head. The captain-general sent one of our men to the giant so that he might perform the same actions as a sign of peace. Having done that, the man led the giant to an islet where the captain-general was waiting. When the giant was in the captain-general's and our presence he marveled greatly, and made signs with one finger raised upward, believing that we had come from the sky. He was so tall that we reached only to his waist, and he was well proportioned.

Then an interesting thing takes place. Here are Pigafetta's words: "The captain caused food and drink to be given to this giant, then they showed him some things, amongst others, a steel mirror. When the giant saw his likeness in it, he was greatly terrified, leaping backwards, and made three or four of our men fall down." (Recent research has demonstrated that even dolphins are able to recognize themselves in a mirror.) Magellan then took two of the Indians captive but they later escaped.

Even before Magellan there is an account of giant Indians in South America in which they are described as "larger than Germans or Hungarians...the footprints left upon the sand show them to have feet twice as large as those of a medium-sized man." This evidently did not relate to Patagonian Indians, though.

Albo makes no mention of their unusual size in his description of these Indians. He writes, "Many Indians came there, who dress in certain skins of the anta, which resemble camels without the hump ... Those Indians are very prudent, swift runners, and very well-built and well-appearing men." Maximilian Transylvanus on the other hand reports that they were "ten spans tall" (about 7 ft, 6 in or 2.3 m). Yet James Weddell, a contemporary of Darwin, liked the Indians but "judged it proper to impress them with an idea of the offence of stealing; and accordingly placed this criminal in the main rigging, and gave him a smart lash with a cat of nine tails, making him understand that it was a punishment for the crime of which he had been gulty." Weddell stated that "this gentle chastisement had the desired effect." The Indians must have been completely demoralized by this behavior.

This is one of the many examples in history of people judging others by their own standards rather than trying to understand the standards of others. Many travelers in today's world still suffer from this same dangerous arrogant attitude.

Until about 1830 the Indians, as a group, suffered no serious interference from the Europeans. But then came the missionaries, the sealers, the sheep farmers, and the gold panners. The missionaries brought disease as well as strict European standards; the sealers brought syphilis; some of the sheep farmers hunted and killed the Indians because the natives stole the sheep; the gold panners simply brought liquor. Such contact between Europeans and the natives was so devastating that the indigenous population became extinct in a very short period of time.

Indians in a missionary camp

Museum Saliesano

There were still many relatively small confrontations between the Indians and the settlers occurring even into the twentieth century. A few settlers were killed but most of the fatalities were natives. Although there were instances of Indians being hunted and killed for no particular reason, there were also many times when Indians were robbing or assaulting the settlers.

Regardless of who was at fault, the end result contributed to the eventual extinction of the Patagonian Indians.

V

PATAGONIA TODAY

Argentina

Argentines are a mixture of diverse national and ethnic groups. Descendants of Italian and Spanish immigrants have predominated since the 16th century, although many other ethnic groups have come to Argentina.

There has been a recent wave of immigrants to Argentina from other Latin American countries, perhaps due to the fact that Argentines enjoy a relatively high standard of living. Half the population considers itself middle class. One-third of the population lives in the greater Buenos Aires area.

In 1502 the first Europeans arrived with the voyage of Amerigo Vespucci. Spaniards settled and exploited the country until 1816 when Buenos Aires formally declared independence from Spain. Subsequently, centralist and federalist groups waged a lengthy conflict between themselves to determine the future of the nation.

National unity finally was established and a constitution created in 1853.

The military intervened repeatedly in the evolution of democracy, most prominently with the rule of Juan Perón. Perón rose to power in 1946. Until 1983, the military continued to dominate the direction of the country. The military's erratic rule culminated in the "dirty war" of 1982. This was a failed attempt to take the Falkland Islands from Britain. It took a fearsome toll in lives lost and human rights violated.

After 1983 Argentina experienced a generally successful and peaceful return to democracy. Reforms have drastically changed the role of the state in Argentine economic life. Notwithstanding the recent economic crisis, Argentina is today a true democracy with an independent judiciary, and the armed forces under civilian control. The Argentine military is now a small, all-volunteer force devoted mainly to international peacekeeping. Cooperation with the U.S. has become an important part of Argentine foreign policy; Argentina was the only Latin American country to participate in the Gulf war.

The exploration of Argentine Patagonia began in 1853, with the expedition led by an Argentine, DonLuisPiedra Buena. He was the one who found the corpses of the companions of missionary Allen Gardiner in Puerto Español. After that Piedra Buena traveled to other parts of Patagonia setting up shelters for stranded seamen. The effort led him to introduce goats on Staten Island (southeast of Tierra del Fuego) so that marooned sailors could find something to eat. Goats still flourish there today.

Piedra Buena attempted to establish a colony on the Strait of Magellan in 1869. The Argentine government failed to come through with the aid they had promised, so the scheme didn't work. The president at the time actually preferred that the "desert southern lands" belong to Chile.

Chile

The Patagonian part of Chile is rich in forests and grazing lands and features a string of volcanoes and lakes. The southern coast is a labyrinth of fjords, inlets, canals, twisting peninsulas, and islands. It also has small, rapidly declining petroleum reserves, which supplied about 8% of Chile's domestic requirements during 1996. Natural resources in the south also include: forest, natural gas, coal, limestone, sheep, and seafood.

About 13,000 years ago, migrating Indians settled in fertile valleys and along the coast of what is now Chile. Less than 500 years ago the Spanish began settlements in Chile. Now it is a Spanish-speaking nation. The drive for independence from Spain was precipitated by usurpation of the Spanish throne by Napoleon's brother Joseph. A national *junta* in the name of

Ferdinand–heir to the deposed king–was formed on September 18, 1810. Spanish attempts to reimpose arbitrary rule during what was called the *Reconquista* led to a prolonged struggle under Bernardo O'Higgins, Chile's most renowned patriot. Chilean independence was formally proclaimed on February 12, 1818. In the 1880s, Chile signed a treaty with Argentina confirming Chilean sovereignty over the Strait of Magellan.

The 1964 presidential election of Christian Democrat Eduardo Frei-Montalva by an absolute majority initiated a period of major reform. Under the slogan "Revolution in Liberty," the Frei Administration embarked on far-reaching social and economic programs, particularly in education, housing, and agrarian reform, including rural unionization of agricultural workers. By 1967, however, Frei encountered increasing opposition from leftists, who charged that his reforms were inadequate, and from conservatives, who found them excessive.

In 1970, Dr.Salvador Allende, a Marxist and member of Chile's Socialist Party, who headed the "Popular Unity" (UP) coalition of Socialists, Communists, Radicals, and dissident Christian Democrats, was elected by a narrow margin. His program included the nationalization of most remaining private industries and banks, massive land expropriation, and collectivization. Allende's proposals also included the nationalization of U.S. interests in Chile's major copper mines. Elected with only 36% of the vote and by a plurality of only 36,000 votes, Allende never enjoyed majority support in the Chilean Congress or broad popular support. Domestic production declined, severe shortages of consumer goods, food, and manufactured products were widespread and inflation reached 1,000% per year. Mass demonstrations, recurring strikes, violence by both government supporters and opponents, and widespread rural unrest ensued in response to the general deterioration of the economy. By 1973, Chilean society had split into two hostile camps. A military coup overthrew Allende on September 11, 1973. As the armed forces bombarded the presidential palace, Allende reportedly committed suicide.

Following the coup in 1973, Chile was ruled by a military regime headed by General Augusto Pinochet. The first years of the regime were marked by serious human rights violations. In its later years, however, the regime gradually permitted some freedom of assembly, speech, and association, and allowed trade-union activity. A plebiscite was held in October, 1988 to determine whether the fifteen-year rule of the military dictatorship under General Pinochet should be extended. Pinochet was voted out and since then Chile has been a democracy.

In contrast to its authoritarian political rule, the military government had pursued decidedly laissez-faire economic policies. During its sixteen years in power, Chile moved toward a largely free-market economy, which fostered an increase in domestic and foreign private investment. In December 1989, Christian Democrat Patricio Aylwin was elected president. In the 1993 election, EduardoFr ei Ruiz-Tagle of the Christian Democratic Party was elected president for a six-year term and took office in March 1994. In 2000, RicardoLagos Escobar became pr esident.

Chile today is divided into thirteen administrative regions, each headed by an administrator appointed by the central government. The regions are divided into forty provinces, each of which is administered by a governor who is also appointed by the central government. The provinces are divided into municipalities headed by appointed mayors.

Chile's judiciary is now independent and includes a court of appeal, a system of military courts, a constitutional tribunal, and the Supreme Court.

Chile's armed forces are subject to civilian control exercised by the president through the Minister of Defense. Under the 1980 constitution, the services enjoy considerable autonomy, and the president cannot remove service commanders on his own authority. The 55,000-person army is organized into six divisions, one separate brigade, and an air wing. The navy consists of 29,000 persons, including 5,200 marines. The fleet of thirty-one surface vessels and four submarines is based in Valparaiso. The navy operates its own aircraft. The air force has a strength of 15,000. Air assets are distributed among four air brigades headquartered in Iquique, Santiago, Puerto Montt, and Punta Arenas. The air force also operates an airbase on King George Island, Antarctica.

Chile has achieved central government budget surpluses every year since 1988. The foreign investment laws offer investors basically the same treatment as domestic firms, along with some extra guarantees.

Chile's 1996 free trade agreement with Canada was modeled largely on NAFTA in anticipation of an eventual trade pact with the United States. The United States is Chile's largest single supplier, supplying 23% of the country's imports in 1997. Chile's credit rating is one of the best in Latin America. With its return to democracy in 1990, Chile became an active participant in the international political arena. Relations between the United States and Chile are better now than at any other time in history. The warm relationship enjoyed by the United States and Chile today contrasts with the difficult period of relations during Augusto Pinochet's military regime from 1973-90.

Chile has about 46.5 persons per sq mi (19 persons per sq km).The country consists of mainly a coast and virtually no interior. The majority of its population of fifteen million is crammed around its capital, Santiago. The north-ern-most third of the country is desert, while the southern-most is Patagonia, a land of mostly un-inhabited fjords and glaciers. The country backs up against the Andes Mountains.

Near the Chilean Andes and along their west-ern flank is one of the world's densest concen-trations of volcanoes, both extinct and active. There are over 2,000, including forty-eight that have erupted at least once within the last one hundred years. The abundance of volcanic fea-tures in Chile and its vicinity is also reflected in the frequent seismic events and conspicuous evi-dence of recent tectonic movements.

Patagonia, A Region of Two Nations

Argentina is an immense country spread out on vast, rolling plains on the other side of the Andes. There are five times as many people there as in Chile. Argentines and Chileans are similar in that they speak Spanish and are descendants of European immigrants. The Chileans have a bit more of a mixture of Indian features, but not as much as in Peru or Mexico. The overwhelming majority in both countries is Roman Catholic. People of both countries are friendly and polite. The citizens are family-oriented, and both like and admire North Americans.

Historically, Argentina and Chile both seem to swing between anarchy and authoritarianism, with Argentina swinging more wildly of the two. The German army has influenced both armies, and the English navy has influenced both navies.

As has been so common in South America, the military of Argentina and Chile took over their governments during the anti-communist hysteria of the Cold War. Unfortunately, the United States government encouraged this. Many people were jailed, tortured, or killed.

Although similar in many respects as a people, Argentines and Chileans are very different as individuals. Argentines are outspoken and optimistic. They tend to be reckless, which is perhaps best demonstrated recently by their 1982

invasion of the Falkland Islands. Chileans, on the
other hand, are more reserved and pessimistic.
Although the two peoples face similar problems in Patagonia, they hardly communicate, and
appear to cooperate only by allowing tourists and
natural gas to cross smoothly from one country
to the other.

Population

Tierra del Fuego has about 115,000 inhabitants today with 70,000 in Argentina and 45,000
in Chile.

On the Argentine side tourism is a major
source of employment with thirty-three hotels
(one five-star and three four-star). It has 10.8%
of the natural gas reserves of the country, and
8% of the oil reserves. Tierra del Fuego (Argentina) has 130 mi (210 km) of paved roads, two
airports (Río Grande and Ushuaia), and five
power plants. The Chilean part of Tierra del
Fuego is less developed than the Argentine side.

As mentioned, prisons have played an important role in the history of Patagonia. Both Punta
Arenas, Chile and Ushuaia, Argentina have
evolved from convict settlements or prisons. The
prisons no longer exist, although during General
Augusto Pinochet's dictatorship in Chile a concentration camp for political prisoners existed on
Dawson Island some forty miles (64 km) south
of Punta Arenas. This terrible camp operated for
over a year in 1973–74. Also, in Pinochet's time

some political prisoners were held in Punta Arenas and elsewhere in Patagonia. It is estimated that 1,000 people were arbitrarily deprived of their liberty and tortured in 1973.

The concentration camp on Dawson Island had earlier been used as a mission camp for the native people. In 1890, the Chilean government had given Salesian missionaries from Italy a 20-year concession on Dawson Island to educate, care for, and adapt indigenous people. Salesian missionaries also operated elsewhere in Patagonia.

GeneralAugusto Pinochet had overthr own the Popular Unity (UP) government of Salvador Allende in 1973. About 30 UP politicians including a former senator and a former cabinet member were sent to Dawson Island following the coup, alongside some 200 prisoners from the local area.

The Dawson Island camp, on a 2,000-square-kilometer tract of land, had a capacity of 1,500 prisoners. But reportedly there were never more than 400 prisoners. The prison had three categories of cells. Level one prisoners were allowed clothing and blankets. Level twos received clothing but no blankets while level threes had neither clothing nor blankets.

Resources

Natural resources include fish, forest products, sheep, and some oil and gas. Industries include home electronics (television sets, video cassette players, car stereos, radios, etc.), textiles, plastics, and canned fish.

Gold has been, and still is, extracted from areas of Patagonia. Evidently gold was discovered in Patagonia sometime before 1867, but a record of who found it or when does not exist. This is different from the famous finding of gold by James Marshall in Sutter's Creek, California in 1848 which everyone soon knew about. Patagonia is so far off the beaten track and so difficult an area in which to maneuver that the historical record is not very complete.

One existing account comes from the year 1876. A noted Argentine sailor, DonGr egorio Ibañez, was stranded near Cape Virgin, at the eastern end of the Strait of Magellan. His shipwrecked crew was digging for water near the surf when they discovered black sand with gold in it. Also, about that time, people were bringing gold out from Las Minas creek near Punta Arenas. In 1884 another shipwreck occurred in the Cape Virgin area. When salvagers arrived from Punta Arenas to scrounge the wreck they began talking about the gold find eight years earlier. Some of the men began digging "just for luck" and again found gold.

News of this find resulted in the Argentine Government sending an engineer to examine the region. His report stated "the gold-bearing sands of Patagonia are richer than those of California and Australia." This report resulted in a number of gold mining claims in Buenos Aires. Unfortunately, most of the people filing claims had never actually been to Patagonia, so many of the claims overlapped. Confusion reigned!

It is reported that one man organized an expedition with sluices, and windmill pumps to fill the sluices with water. But most of the gold was in the beach sand, which was under water at high tide. The windmills would not pump when the wind didn't blow—and when it did, the waves prevented the men from supplying sand to the sluices. So that effort failed.

Further mining took place in various locations on the island of Tierra del Fuego and near Punta Arenas. It was only mildly successful. Most of Patagonia's gold lies in the beach sands, which in some areas is replenished by storms. Gold is still being taken out today near Porvenir and, perhaps, can still be found elsewhere in Patagonia. But it remains very difficult to extract.

Investors

The investment and plans of the Trillium Corporation of Bellingham, Washington have raised a major fuss recently. Trillium's Río Condor project involves a $200 million (US) investment in the logging of 257,000 hectares (625,000 acres) of lenga on Tierra del Fuego. The project has enjoyed the support of the Chilean government.

The forest was initially sold under the dictatorship of GeneralAugusto Pinochet (1973–90) at the absurdly low price of a $1 per hectare (a hectare is 2.47 acres). The sale was later renegotiated for $3 per hectare. Local officials have been looking forward for years to the 150 jobs the project would create.

However, Greenpeace and several other environmental groups have opposed the project and it is still in limbo. There have been several court actions concerning the issue. Environmental groups and some politicians are opposed to the project due to the impact it would have on the endangered lenga tree, and the fragile ecosystem of Tierra del Fuego. Trillium plans to produce wood chips, which are used in the manufacturing of hardboard and "green-friendly" packaging.

It has been pointed out before that the lenga tree grows very slowly due to the cold of Tierra del Fuego, and thus replenishing the forest would be a lengthy process. Another argument against the Río Condor project is that the timber industry in Chile has a very poor record as far as contributing to the problems of unemployment and poverty.

Trillium also owns 75,000 acres (30,050 hectares) in Argentina and their project there has also aroused the ire of environmentalists. The citizens of Ushuaia, at least, have succeeded in prohibiting the manufacture of wood chips in their area.

Another U.S. corporation, Boise Cascade, also has a chip mill project in Southern Chile, which, environmentalists maintain, will double the rate of deforestation in Chile's ancient temperate rainforests.

In 1968 Yvon Chouinard and Doug Tompkins climbed mountains in Patagonia and fell in love with the region. Chouinard went on to establish a very successful outdoor clothing company which he named Patagonia. Tompkins amassed a fortune from another clothing chain, Esprit.

Tompkins, in the '90s, returned to Patagonia with the dream of establishing the world's largest private park in Chilean Patagonia, running from the ocean to the Argentine border. His goal is protection of the fragile environment; he promises to return the land eventually to the Chilean national park system. At least one major environmental group supports his effort, but the Chilean government is concerned. At one point they said they would buy the land themselves but later backed down from that pledge (or threat, depending on how you look at it.)

The Chilean government's concern was apparently based on the fact that his park would take considerable land out of use for growing timber. Tompkins owns 667,000 acres (270,000 hectares) and eventually intends to own 900,000 acres (364,000 hectares). This is about the size of Rhode Island. Also there is anxiety about a foreigner owning this much land. His land nearly divides the country in two!

Recently Tompkins' wife, Kris McDivitt, purchased a 128,000 acre (52,000 hectare) sheep ranch in Argentina. She is the former CEO of the outdoor clothing company, Patagonia, founded by Tompkins old pal, Yvon Chouinard. Ms. McDivitt may transfer her sheep ranch to the Argentine National Park System very soon. Her land is not as controversial as her husband's as it is not wooded and is relatively small. Not surprisingly, the Argentine government welcomes her investment.

Yvon Chouinard, who is on the board of the non-profit organization Ms. McDivitt has created, is quoted as saying, "We've been using Patagonia's name for twenty-five years. This is a kind of royalty payment."

Investors from around the world have been buying up land in the Argentine portion of Patagonia. In recent years, Ted Turner has purchased an 11,000 acre (4,450 hectare) ranch called La Primavera (Springtime). He was quoted as saying, "We chose it because there isn't a more beautiful place in the world."

The British restaurateur, Charlie Lewis, who owns the South American franchise for Planet Hollywood and Hard Rock Café, purchased a 32,000 acre (13,000 hectare) ranch. Luciano Benetton, the Italian fashion magnate, in 1991 purchased 2.2 million acres (890,000 hectares) and George Soros bought over 1 million acres (405,000 hectares) and a luxury hotel in the

Argentine town of Bariloche. Benetton and Soros are now two of Argentina's biggest landowners. Other celebrity landowners reportedly include Sylvester Stallone, the movie star. According to one report from 1998, Patagonian real estate carried an average price of $20 an acre.

Early investors included Butch Cassidy and the Sundance Kid. They bought a 12,000 acre (4,900 hectare) ranch with loot from the 1900 robbery of the First National Bank in Winnemucca, Nevada. Cassidy wrote to a friend, "I visited the best cities and best parts of South America till I got here. And this part of the country looked so good that I located, and I think for good."

However, it wasn't long before the pair went back to bank robbing and were soon killed in Bolivia.

Archaeology and Palaeontology

In 1997, scientists found a nest of dinosaur eggs in a remote area of Patagonia. The nest proved to be from a sauropod, a large dinosaur who lived about eighty million years ago.

More recently, other major finds have rocked the scientific world. Patagonia has become one of the major archeological areas of the world. The archeological wonders of Patagonia include the discovery of a fossil of a platypus tooth. The platypus, a strange- looking egg-laying mammal, exists today only in Australia. Some 63 million years ago Australia, Antarctica, and South America were one continent, known as Gondwana. This is the explanation for the platypus tooth being found in Patagonia.

A French speleologist, Jean-Francois Pernette, has explored the caves in some of the islands off the western coast of southern Chile. Though fantastic caves were investigated, the primary findings were that research is extremely difficult in this part of Patagonia. The Cueva de las Manos (Cave of the Hands) in Patagonia has a number of cave paintings which date back some 10,000 years.

Nearby Lands

The Falkland Islands are a group of English-owned islands some 350 mi (560 km) east of Patagonia in the south Atlantic. The Falklands provided the base for some of the early missionary-sponsored attempts to settle Patagonia. In 1982, Argentina tried to take these islands (which the Argentines call the Malvinas.) They had long laid claim to these islands. The resulting war lasted a little over two months.

About 20 mi (32 km) off the southeastern tip of Patagonia is Staten Island (*Isla de los Estados*). It is mentioned occasionally in the accounts of early voyages. The other Staten Island (part of New York City) is 7,000 mi (11,000 km) to the north.

Antartica is some 525 mi (845 km) south of Patagonia. It is the fifth-largest continent, following Asia, Africa, North America, and South America, larger than Australia and Europe. In area it is 5,400,000 sq mi (14 million sq km) or slightly less than 1.5 times the size of the United States. It is 98% covered in ice.

It has research stations from some twenty-nine nations, all signers of the Antarctic Treaty. The treaty, which went into effect in 1961, establishes the legal framework for the management of Antarctica. The treaty contains a number of provisions that protect the environment and international status of the continent. It neither recognizes nor repudiates the existing national claims, but denies any future claims.

As of 1999, there are forty-four treaty-member-nations including the seven nations (of course Argentina and Chile are two of them) that claim portions of Antarctica as national territory (some claims overlap). The United States and some other nations that have made no claims have reserved the right to do so.

Afterword

Patagonia is one of the most unspoiled, and yet beautiful, areas of the world. Whether you choose to visit or simply become a fan of this region you will be embarking on an adventure that is virtually unparalleled in its variety. From the tree-covered slopes of the Andes in Torres del Paine National Park to the violent seas around Cape Horn and from the pampas of Argentina to the glaciers of Beagle Channel this is a varied, dramatic, and unique land.

If you're a history buff, you will find the tales of the Tehuelche giants and the rigors of the sailing explorations of Magellan, Drake, and others to be fascinating. Enjoy your personal voyage!

APPENDIX

Darwin, in his *Voyage of the Beagle* had this to say:

In the end of May, 1834, we entered for a second time the eastern mouth of the Strait of Magellan. The country on both sides of this part of the Strait consists of nearly level plains, like those of Patagonia. Cape Negro, a little within the second Narrows, may be considered as the point where the land begins to assume the marked features of Tierra del Fuego. On the East Coast, south of the Strait, broken park-like scenery in a like manner connects these two countries, which are opposed to each other in almost every feature. It is truly surprising to find in a space of twenty miles such a change in the landscape. If we take a rather greater distance, as between Port Famine and Gregory Bay, that is about sixty miles, the difference is still more wonderful. At the former place, we have rounded mountains concealed by impervious forests, which are drenched with the rain, brought by an endless succession

*of gales; while at Cape Gregory, there
is a clear and bright blue sky over the
dry and sterile plains. The atmospheric
currents, although rapid, turbulent,
and unconfined by any apparent limits, yet seem to follow, like a river in
its bed, a regularly determined course.*

*June 1st. — We anchored in the fine
bay of Port Famine. It was now the
beginning of winter, and I never saw
a more cheerless prospect; the dusky
woods, piebald with snow, could be
only seen indistinctly, through a driz-
zling hazy atmosphere. We were, however, lucky in getting two fine days.
On one of these, Mount Sarmiento, a
distant mountain 6800 feet high, pre-
sented a very noble spectacle. I was frequently surprised in the scenery of
Tierra del Fuego, at the little apparent
elevation of mountains really lofty. I
suspect it is owing to a cause which
would not at first be imagined, namely,
that the whole mass, from the summit
to the water's edge, is generally in full
view. I remember having seen a mountain, first from the Beagle Channel,
where the whole sweep from the summit to the base was full in view, and
then from Ponsonby Sound across*

several successive ridges; and it was curious to observe in the latter case, as each fresh ridge afforded fresh means of judging of the distance, how the mountain rose in height.

When the Beagle was here in the month of February, I started one morning at four o'clock to ascend Mount Tarn, which is 2600 feet high, and is the most elevated point in this immediate district. We went in a boat to the foot of the mountain (but unluckily not to the best part), and then began our ascent. The forest commences at the line of high-water mark, and during the first two hours I gave over all hopes of reaching the summit. So thick was the wood, that it was necessary to have constant recourse to the compass; for every landmark, though in a mountainous country, was completely shut out. In the deep ravines, the death-like scene of desolation exceeded all description; outside it was blowing a gale, but in these hollows, not even a breath of wind stirred the leaves of the tallest trees. So gloomy, cold, and wet was every part, that not even the fungi, mosses, or ferns could flourish. In the valleys it was scarcely possible to crawl

along, they were so completely barri-
caded by great mouldering trunks,
which had fallen down in every direc-
tion. When passing over these natural
bridges, one's course was often arrested
by sinking knee deep into the rotten
wood; at other times, when attempt-
ing to lean against a firm tree, one was
startled by finding a mass of decayed
matter ready to fall at the slightest
touch. We at last found ourselves
among the stunted trees, and then soon
reached the bare ridge, which con-
ducted us to the summit. Here was a
view characteristic of Tierra del Fuego;
irregular chains of hills, mottled with
patches of snow, deep yellowish-green
valleys, and arms of the sea intersect-
ing the land in many directions. The
strong wind was piercingly cold, and
the atmosphere rather hazy, so that we
did not stay long on the top of the
mountain. Our descent was not quite
so laborious as our ascent, for the
weight of the body forced a passage,
and all the slips and falls were in the
right direction.

I have already mentioned the sombre
and dull character of the evergreen for-
ests, in which two or three species of

trees grow, to the exclusion of all others. Above the forest land, there are many dwarf alpine plants, which all spring from the mass of peat, and help to compose it. These plants are very remarkable from their close alliance with the species growing on the mountains of Europe, though so many thousand miles distant. The central part of Tierra del Fuego, where the clay-slate formation occurs, is most favourable to the growth of trees; on the outer coast the poorer granitic soil, and a situation more exposed to the violent winds, do not allow of their attaining any great size. Near Port Famine I have seen more large trees than anywhere else: I measured a Winter's Bark which was four feet six inches in girth, and several of the beech were as much as thirteen feet. Captain King also mentions a beech which was seven feet in diameter, seventeen feet above the roots.

There is one vegetable production deserving notice from its importance as an article of food to the Fuegians. It is a globular, bright-yellow fungus, which grows in vast numbers on the beech-trees. When young it is elastic and turgid, with a smooth surface; but when mature it shrinks, becomes tougher, and has its entire surface deeply pitted or honey-combed... This fungus belongs to a new and curious genus, I found a second species on another species of beech in Chile... How singular is this relationship between parasitical fungi and the trees on which they grow, in distant parts of the world! In Tierra del Fuego the fungus in its tough and mature state is collected in large quantities by the women and children, and is eaten un-cooked. It has a mucilaginous, slightly sweet taste, with a faint smell like that of a mushroom. With the exception of a few berries, chiefly of a dwarf arbutus, the natives eat no vegetable food besides this fungus. In New Zealand, before the introduction of the potato, the roots of the fern were largely consumed; at the present time, I believe, Tierra del Fuego is the only country in the world where a cryptogamic plant affords a staple article of food.

The zoology of Tierra del Fuego, as might have been expected from the nature of its climate and vegetation, is very poor. Of mammalia, besides whales and seals, there is one bat, a kind of mouse (Reithrodon chinchilloides), two true mice, a ctenomys allied to or identical with the tucutuco, two foxes (Canis Magellanicus and C. Azarae), a sea-otter, the guanaco, and a deer. Most of these animals inhabit only the drier eastern parts of the country; and the deer has never been seen south of the Strait of Magellan. Observing the general correspondence of the cliffs of soft sandstone, mud, and shingle, on the opposite sides of the Strait, and on some intervening islands, one is strongly tempted to believe that the land was once joined, and thus allowed animals so delicate and helpless as the tucutuco and Reithrodon to pass over. The correspondence of the cliffs is far from proving any junction; because such cliffs generally are formed by the intersection of sloping deposits, which, before the elevation of the land, had been accumulated near the then existing shores. It is, however, a remarkable coincidence, that in the two large islands cut off by the Beagle Channel from the rest of Tierra del Fuego, one has cliffs composed of matter that may be called stratified alluvium, which front similar ones on the opposite side of the channel, — while the other is exclusively bordered by old crystalline rocks: in the former, called Navarin Island, both foxes and guanacos occur; but in the latter, Hoste Island, although similar in every respect, and only separated by a channel a little more than half a mile wide, I have the word of Jemmy Button for saying that neither of these animals are found.

The gloomy woods are inhabited by few birds... if we turn from the land to the sea, we shall find the latter as abundantly stocked with living creatures as the former is poorly so. In all parts of the world a rocky and partially protected shore perhaps supports, in a given space, a greater number of individual animals than any other station. There is one marine production which, from its importance, is worthy of a particular history. It is the kelp, or Macrocystis pyrifera. This plant grows on every rock from low-water mark to a great depth, both on the outer coast and within the channels. I believe, during the voyages of the Adventure and Beagle, not one rock near the surface was discovered which was not buoyed *by this floating weed. The good service it thus affords to vessels navigating near this stormy land is evident; and it certainly has saved many a one from being wrecked. I know few things more surprising than to see this plant growing and flourishing amidst those great breakers of the western ocean, which no mass of rock, let it be ever so hard, can long resist. The stem is round, slimy, and smooth, and seldom has a diameter of so much as an inch. A few taken together are sufficiently strong to support the weight of the large loose stones, to which in the inland channels they grow attached; and yet some of these stones were so heavy that when drawn to the surface, they could scarcely be lifted into a boat by one person. Captain Cook, in his second voyage, says, that this plant at Kerguelen Land rises from a greater depth than twenty-four fathoms; "and as it does not grow in a perpendicular direction, but makes a very acute angle with the bottom, and much of it afterwards spreads many fathoms on the surface of the sea, I am well warranted to say that some of it grows to the length of sixty fathoms and upwards." I do not suppose the stem of any other plant attains so great a length as three hundred and sixty feet, as stated by Captain Cook. Captain FitzRoy, moreover, found it growing up from the greater depth of forty-five fathoms. The beds of this sea-weed, even when of not great breadth, make excellent natural floating breakwaters. It is quite curious to see, in an exposed harbour, how soon the waves from the open sea, as they travel through the straggling stems, sink in height, and pass into smooth water.*

The number of living creatures of all Orders, whose existence intimately depends on the kelp, is wonderful. A great volume might be written, describing the inhabitants of one of these beds of sea-weed. ... Often as I recurred to a branch of the kelp, I never failed to discover animals of new and curious structures. ... I can only compare these great aquatic forests of the southern hemisphere with the terrestrial ones in the intertropical regions. Yet if in any country a forest was destroyed, I do not believe nearly so many species of animals would perish as would here, from the destruction of the kelp. Amidst the leaves of this plant numerous species of fish live, which nowhere else could find food or shelter; with their destruction the many cormorants and other fishing birds, the otters, seals, and porpoises, would soon perish also; and lastly, the Fuegian savage, the miserable lord of this miserable land, would redouble his cannibal feast, decrease in numbers, and perhaps cease to exist.

June 8th. — We weighed anchor early in the morning and left Port Famine. Captain Fitz Roy determined to leave the Strait of Magellan by the Magdalen Channel, which had not long been discovered. Our course lay due south, down that gloomy passage which I have before alluded to as appearing to lead to another and worse world. The wind was fair, but the atmosphere was very thick; so that we missed much curious scenery. The dark ragged clouds were rapidly driven over the mountains, from their summits nearly down to their bases. The glimpses which we caught through the dusky mass were highly interesting; jagged points, cones of snow, blue glaciers, strong outlines, marked on a lurid sky, were seen at different distances and heights. In the midst of such scenery we anchored at Cape Turn, close to Mount Sarmiento, which was then hidden in the clouds. At the base of the lofty and almost perpendicular sides of our little cove there was one deserted wigwam, and it alone reminded us that man sometimes wandered into these desolate regions. But it would be difficult to imagine a scene where he seemed to have fewer claims or less authority. The inanimate works of nature — rock, ice, snow, wind, and water — all warring with each other, yet combined against man — here reigned in absolute sovereignty.

June 9th. — In the morning we were delighted by seeing the veil of mist gradually rise from Sarmiento, and display it to our view. This mountain, which is one of the highest in Tierra del Fuego, has an altitude of 6800 feet. Its base, for about an eighth of its total height, is clothed by dusky woods, and above this a field of snow extends to the summit. These vast piles of snow, which never melt, and seem destined to last as long as the world holds together, present a noble and even sublime spectacle. The outline of the mountain was admirably clear and defined. Owing to the abundance of light reflected from the white and glittering surface, no shadows were cast on any part; and those lines which intersected the sky could alone be distinguished: hence the mass stood out in the boldest relief. Several glaciers descended in a winding course from the upper great expanse of snow to the sea-coast: they may be likened to great frozen Niagaras; and perhaps these cataracts of blue ice are full as beautiful as the moving ones of water. By night we reached the western part of the channel; but the water was so deep that no anchorage could be found. We were in consequence obliged to stand off and on in this narrow arm of the sea, during a pitch-dark night of fourteen hours long.

June 10th. — In the morning we made the best of our way into the open Pacific. The western coast generally consists of low, rounded, quite barren hills of granite and greenstone. Sir J. Narborough called one part South Desolation, because it is "so desolate a land to behold:" and well indeed might he say so. Outside the main islands, there are numberless scattered rocks on which the long swell of the open ocean incessantly rages. We passed out between the East and West Furies; and a little farther northward there are so many breakers that the sea is called the Milky Way. One sight of such a coast is enough to make a landsman dream for a week about shipwrecks, peril, and death; and with this sight we bade farewell forever to Tierra del Fuego...

The equable, humid, and windy climate of Tierra del Fuego extends, with only a small increase of heat, for many degrees along the West Coast of the continent. The forests for 600 miles northward of Cape Horn, have a very similar aspect. As a proof of the equable climate, even for 300 or 400 miles still further northward, I may mention that in Chiloe (corresponding in latitude with the northern parts of Spain) the peach seldom produces fruit, whilst strawberries and apples thrive to perfection. Even the crops of barley and wheat are often brought into the houses to be dried and ripened. At Valdivia (in the same latitude of 40°, with Madrid) grapes and figs ripen, but are not common; olives seldom ripen even partially, and oranges not at all. These fruits, in corresponding latitudes in Europe, are well known to succeed to perfection; and even in this continent, at the Rio Negro, under nearly the same parallel with Valdivia, sweet potatoes (convolvulus) are cultivated; and grapes, figs, olives, oranges, water and musk melons, produce abundant fruit. Although the humid and equable climate of Chiloe, and of the coast northward and southward of it, is so unfavourable to our fruits, yet the native forests, from lat. 45 to 38°, almost rival in luxuriance those of the glowing intertropical regions. Stately trees of many kinds, with smooth and highly coloured barks, are loaded by parasitical monocotyledonous plants; large and elegant ferns are numerous, and arborescent grasses entwine the trees into one entangled mass to the height of thirty or forty feet above the ground. Palm-trees grow in lat 37°; an arborescent grass, very like a bamboo, in 40°; and another closely allied kind, of great length, but not erect, flourishes even as far south as 45° S.

An equable climate, evidently due to the large area of sea compared with the land, seems to extend over the greater part of the Southern Hemisphere; and, as a consequence, the vegetation partakes of a semi-tropical character...

As the height of the plane of perpetual snow seems chiefly to be determined by the extreme heat of the summer, rather than by the mean temperature of the year, we ought not to be surprised at its descent in the Strait of Magellan, where the summer is so cool, to only 3500 or 4000 feet above the level of the sea; although in Norway, we must travel to between lat. 67 and 70° N., that is, about 14° nearer the pole, to meet with perpetual snow at this low level. The difference in height, namely, about 9000 feet, between the snow-line on the Cordillera behind Chiloe (with its highest points ranging from only 5600 to 7500 feet) and in central Chile (a distance of only 9° of latitude), is truly wonderful. The land from the southward of Chiloe to near Concepcion (lat. 37°) is hidden by one dense forest dripping with moisture. The sky is cloudy, and we have seen how badly the fruits of southern Europe succeed. In central Chile, on the other hand, a little northward of Concepcion, the sky is generally clear,

*rain does not fall for the seven sum-
mer months, and southern European
fruits succeed admirably; and even the
sugar-cane has been cultivated. No
doubt the plane of perpetual snow un-
dergoes the above remarkable flexure
of 9000 feet, unparalleled in other parts
of the world, not far from the latitude
of Concepcion, where the land ceases
to be covered with forest-trees; for trees
in South America indicate a rainy climate, and rain a clouded sky and little
heat in summer.*

*The descent of glaciers to the sea must,
I conceive, mainly depend (subject, of
course, to a proper supply of snow in
the upper region) on the lowness of the
line of perpetual snow on steep mountains near the coast. As the snow-line
is so low in Tierra del Fuego, we might
have expected that many of the glaciers
would have reached the sea. Nevertheless, I was astonished when I first saw
a range, only from 3000 to 4000 feet
in height, in the latitude of
Cumberland, with every valley filled
with streams of ice descending to the
sea-coast. Almost every arm of the sea,
which penetrates to the interior higher
chain, not only in Tierra del Fuego, but*

*on the coast for 650 miles northwards,
is terminated by "tremendous and as-
tonishing glaciers," as described by one
of the officers on the survey. Great
masses of ice frequently fall from these
icy cliffs, and the crash reverberates
like the broadside of a man-of-war
through the lonely channels. These
falls... produce great waves which
break on the adjoining coasts. It is
known that earthquakes frequently
cause masses of earth to fall from sea-
cliffs: how terrific, then, would be the
effect of a severe shock (and such occur here) on a body like a glacier, already in motion, and traversed by fis-
sures! I can readily believe that the
water would be fairly beaten back out
of the deepest channel, and then, returning with an overwhelming force,
would whirl about huge masses of rock
like so much chaff. In Eyre's Sound, in
the latitude of Paris, there are immense
glaciers, and yet the loftiest
neighbouring mountain is only 6200
feet high. In this Sound, about fifty
icebergs were seen at one time floating
outwards, and one of them must have
been at least 168 feet in total height.
Some of the icebergs were loaded with
blocks of no inconsiderable size, of*

granite and other rocks, different from the clay-slate of the surrounding mountains. The glacier furthest from the pole, surveyed during the voyages of the Adventure and Beagle, is in lat. 46° 50', in the Gulf of Penas. It is 15 miles long, and in one part 7 broad and descends to the sea-coast. But even a few miles northward of this glacier, in Laguna de San Rafael, some Spanish missionaries encountered "many icebergs, some great, some small, and others middle-sized," in a narrow arm of the sea, on the 22nd of the month corresponding with our June, and in a latitude corresponding with that of the Lake of Geneva!

In Europe, the most southern glacier which comes down to the sea is met with, according to Von Buch, on the coast of Norway, in lat. 67° Now, this is more than 20° of latitude, or 1230 miles, nearer the pole than the Laguna de San Rafael. The position of the glaciers at this place and in the Gulf of Penas may be put even in a more striking point of view, for they descend to the sea-coast within 7.5° of latitude, or 450 miles, of a harbour, where three species of Oliva, a Voluta, and a

Terebra, are the commonest shells, within less than 9° from where palms grow, within 4.5° of a region where the jaguar and puma range over the plains, less than 2.5° from arborescent grasses, and (looking to the westward in the same hemisphere) less than 2° from orchideous parasites, and within a single degree of tree-ferns!

These facts are of high geological interest with respect to the climate of the northern hemisphere at the period when boulders were transported. I will not here detail how simply the theory of icebergs being charged with fragments of rock, explain the origin and position of the gigantic boulders of eastern Tierra del Fuego, on the high plain of Santa Cruz, and on the island of Chiloe. In Tierra del Fuego, the greater number of boulders lie on the lines of old sea-channels, now converted into dry valleys by the elevation of the land. They are associated with a great unstratified formation of mud and sand, containing rounded and angular fragments of all sizes, which has originated in the repeated ploughing up of the sea-bottom by the stranding of icebergs, and by the matter transported on them. Few geologists now doubt that those erratic boulders which lie near lofty mountains have been pushed forward by the glaciers themselves, and that those distant from mountains, and embedded in subaqueous deposits, have been conveyed thither either on icebergs or frozen in coast-ice. The connection between the transportal of boulders and the presence of ice in some form, is strikingly shown by their geographical distribution over the earth. In South America they are not found further than 48° of latitude, measured from the southern pole; in North America it appears that the limit of their transportal extends to 53.5° from the northern pole; but in Europe to not more than 40° of latitude, measured from the same point...

On the northern continents, the winter is rendered excessively cold by the radiation from a large area of land into a clear sky, nor is it moderated by the warmth-bringing currents of the sea; the short summer, on the other hand, is hot. In the Southern Ocean the winter is not so excessively cold, but the summer is far less hot, for the clouded

*sky seldom allows the sun to warm the
ocean, itself a bad absorbent of heat:
and hence the mean temperature of the
year…is low.*

*… it is known that in the shallow sea
on the Arctic coast of America the bottom freezes, and does not thaw in
spring so soon as the surface of the
land, moreover at greater depths,
where the bottom of the sea does not
freeze the mud a few feet beneath the
top layer might remain even in summer below 32°, as in the case on the
land with the soil at the depth of a few
feet.*

BIBLIOGRAPHY

Many of the facts in this book came from sites on the World Wide Web. Due to the ephemeral nature of the Internet no effort has been made to list them. Here are additional reliable sources.

Alder, Lin. "A Good Deal on Patagonia," *National Geographic Adventure*, 3, no. 6 (November/ December 2001): 36.

Andrews, Michael. *The Flight of the Condor*. Boston: Little, Brown & Company, 1982.

Beccaceci, Marcelo D. *Natural Patagonia*. St. Paul: Pangaea, 1998.

Bitschene, Peter Rene and José Mendia, Editors. *The August 1991 Eruption of the Hudson Volcano (Patagonian Andes): A Thousand Days After*. Gottingen, Germany: Cuvillier, 1995.

Bourne, Benjamin Franklin. *The Captive in Patagonia: Life Among the Giants*. Boston: Gould & Lincoln, 1853.

Bridges, E. Lucas. *Uttermost Part of the Earth*. New York: E.P. Dutton, 1950.

Bridges, Thomas. *Yamana-English Dictionary*. Buenos Aires: Zagier & Urruty Publications, 1987 (originally printed in 1933).

Burford, Tim. *Chile and Argentina, Backpacking and Hiking*. Old Saybrook, Connecticut: The Globe Pequot Press, 1998.

Cameron, Ian. *Magellan and the First Circumnavigation of the World*. New York: Saturday Review Press, 1973.

Campbell, John. *In Darwin's Wake: Revisiting Beagle's South American Anchorages*. Dobbs Ferry, New York: Sheridan House, 1997.

Chatwin, Bruce and Paul Theroux. *Patagonia Revisited*. Boston: Houghton Mifflin, 1986. (This book was republished with photos by Jeff Gnass under the title *Nowhere is a Place*,) San Francisco: Sierra Club Books, 1992.

Chatwin, Bruce. *In Patagonia*. London: Pan Books, Ltd., 1980.

Chichester, Sir Francis. *Gypsy Moth Circles The World*. New York: Coward-McCann, Inc., 1967.

Couve, Enrique and Claudio Vidal-Ojeda. *Birds of the Beagle Channel*. Punta Arenas, Chile: Fantastico Sur Birding Ltda., 2000.

Dana, Richard Henry, Jr. *Two Years Before the Mast: A Personal Narrative of Life at Sea*. 1840. Reprint, New York: The Heritage Press, 1947.

Darwin, Charles. *The Voyage of the Beagle*. 1845. Reprint, New York: P.F. Collier & Son, 1909.

"Dinosaurs in the Dust." *Newsweek*, 135, no. 2, (July 12, 1999): 44–5.

Dixie, Lady Florence. *Across Patagonia*. New York: Worthington Company, 1880.

Farndon, John. *Dictionary of the Earth*. London and New York: Dorling Kindersley, 1994.

Gamundi, Irma J. and Egon Horak. *Fungi of the Andean-Patagonian Forests*. Buenos Aires: Vasquez Mazzini Editores, 1995.

Garay N., Gladys and Guineo N., Oscar. *Torres del Paine Fauna-Flora and Mountains*. Punta Arenas, Chile: 1997.

Harrison, John. *Where The Earth Ends: a journey beyond patagonia*. London: John Murray (Publishers) Ltd., 2000.

Henderson, James D.,Helen Delpar, and Maurice P. Brungart. *A Reference Guide to Latin American History*. M.E. Sharpe, New York & London, England, 2000.

Hopkins, Robert S. *Darwin's South America*. New York: The John Day Company, 1969.

Hough, Richard. *Captain James Cook*. London, Hodder and Stoughton, 1994.

Hough, Richard. *The Blind Horn's Hate*. New York: W.W. Norton & Co.,1971.

Hudson, W.H. *Idle Days in Patagonia*. London: J.M. Dent & Sons, 1893, last republished in 1954.

"Huevos Dinosaurus," *Discover*, 20, no. 2, (February, 1999): 24.

Lindenmayer, Clem. *Trekking in the Patagonian Andes*. Oakland, California: Lonely Planet, 1998.

Lloyd, Christopher, ed. *The Voyages of Captain James Cook Round the World*. New York: Chanticleer Press, 1949.

Marks, Richard Lee. *Three Men of the Beagle*. New York: Alfred A. Knopf, 1991.

McEwan, Colin, Luis A. Borrero, and Alfredo Prieto, editors. *Patagonia: Natural History, Prehistory and Ethnography at the Uttermost End of the Earth.* Princeton, N.J.: Princeton University Press, 1997.

Menéndez, Enrique Campos. *Soul of the Wind.* Punta Arenas, Chile: Southern Patagonia Publications, 1999.

Morris, Isaac. *A Narrative of the danger & distresses which befell Isaac Morris....* London: S. Birt, 1750(?).

Nancul, Gladys Garay and Oscar Guineo Nenen. *Torres del Paine: Fauna-Flora and Mountains.* Punta Arenas, Chile, 1997.

Perich Slater, José. *Indigenous Extinction in Patagonia.* Punta Arenas, Chile: Impresos Vanic Ltda., 1997.

Peter, Carsten. "Probing Chile's Wild Coast," *National Geographic*, 199, no. 6, (June 2001): 2–19.

Pigafetta, Antonio. *The Voyage of Magellan.* 1525, translation by Paula Spurlin Paige, Englewood, New Jersey: Prentice-Hall, 1969.

Pigafetta, Antonio. *The First Voyage Around the World, An Account of Magellan's Expedition.* edited by Theodore J. Cachey, Jr., New York: Marsilio Publishers, 1995.

Porter, Captain David. *Journal of a Cruise Made to the Pacific Ocean.* Two volumes, second edition, New York, Wiley & Halsted, 1822, reprint, Upper Saddle River, New Jersey: Gregg Press, 1970.

Prieto, Alfredo and Rodrigo Cardenas. *Introduction to Ethnical Photography in Patagonia.* Punta Arenas, Chile: Patagonia Comunicaciones, 1997.

Public Broadcasting Service. *Hidden Worlds, Patagonia's Tuxedo Junction.* Partridge Films, Ltd., 1995. Videocasette.

Rice, Larry. *Baja to Patagonia.* Golden, Colorado: Fulcrum, 1993.

Riesenberg, Felix. *Cape Horn.* New York: Dodd, Mead and Company, 1939.

"Sequels to a Patagonian Journal," *Américas*, 52, no. 2 (March/April 2000): 6–13.

Shipton, Eric. *Tierra del Fuego: the Fatal Lodestone.* London & Tunbridge: Charles Knight & Co. Ltd., 1973.

Spears, John. *The Gold Diggings of Cape Horn*. New York & London, G.P. Putnam's Sons, 1895.

Stanley of Adderley, Lord. *The First Voyage Round the World by Magellan*, 1874, Hakluyt Society, Reprint New York: Burt Franklin, Publisher, no date.

Stephens, Walter. *Giants in Those Days: Folklore, Ancient History, and Nationalism*. Lincoln, Nebraska: University of Nebraska Press, 1989.

Theroux, Paul. *The Old Patagonian Express*. Boston: Houghton Mifflin Company, 1979.

Urruty, Emilio. *The First Adventure Handbook of Southern South America*. Miami and Buenos Aires: Zagier & Urruty Publications, 1992.

Vairo, Carlos Pedro. *Ushuaia*. Ushuaia, Argentina and Buenos Aires: Zagier & Urruty Publications, 1998.

Vairo, Carlos Pedro. *Shipwrecks in Cape Horn, Magallanes, Mitre Peninsula, Malvinas, and South Georgias*. Ushuaia, Argentina and Buenos Aires: Zagier & Urruty Publications, 2001.

Index

A

ablation 45
Africa 32, 99, 110, 112, 167
Ainsworth Bay. 3
airports 158
Alacaluf 103, 114, 123, 125, 130, 131 134, 138-140
albatross(es) 84, 107
Albo 146
alcohol 137
Alexandria 97
Allende, Dr.Salvador 152, 153,159
alpaca 50, 51
American black cherry 86
Americas 99, 127
Amerigo Vespucci 149
Ancient Britons. 131
Andean condor(s) 6, 8, 14, 18, 71-74
Andes 11, 23, 33, 40, 52, 73, 76, 80, 156, 157, 168
anta 146
Antarctic Islands 65
Antarctic Treaty 68, 167
Antarctica 2, 32, 166, 167
anthropologists 140
Antichthon 113
Antipodeans 113
Aónikenk 128, 133
apron 135
araucaria tree 128
Argentina 4, 9, 11, 22-24, 26, 28, 29, 40, 41, 46, 52, 53, 60, 61, 76, 80, 87, 91, 128, 149, 150, 152, 157, 158, 162, 164-168
Argentine National Park System 164
Asia 167
Atlantic 23, 32, 36, 40, 47, 100, 107, 110, 112, 166
Austral Pacific current 49
Austral Parakeet(s) 17, 83
Australia 64, 161, 165- 167
avalanches 5
Avenue of the Glaciers 7, 8, 12
axe 136
Aylwin, Patricio 154

B

backpacking, 51
Bahía Félix 46
Baja California 65
baleen whales 64
Bariloche 165
beachmasters. 65
Beagle 106, 111, 122, 124 137
Beagle Channel 6-9, 11, 12, 14, 23, 25, 40, 41, 47, 49, 83, 121, 134, 168
bears 59
beaver(s) 4, 10, 11, 24, 59-61
beaver dam 4, 9
beaver pelts 60
beef 53
Bellingham, Washington 161
Benetton, Luciano 164, 165
berries. 132
black-necked swan(s) 15, 19, 83
Bligh, William 38, 109, 110

Boat Memory 123, 124
Boise Cascade 163
bola(s) 54, 132, 133, 139
Bolivia 76, 80, 165
Boston 36
Bounty 109
Bourne, BenjaminFranklin
    38, 115
bows and arrows 132
Braun-Menendez Regional
    Museum 27
Brazil 80, 109
Bridges, Lucas, 25, 131
Bridges, Thomas 9, 26, 118,
    121, 135, 137
Britain 150
British Columbia 56
British Empire 115
Brooks Bay 4, 6
Brooks Glacier 3, 4
Buena, DonLuisPiedra 150
Buenos Aires 91, 149, 161

C

Calafate 85
California 36, 65, 160
California Gold Rush 27
callosities 64
Cambiazo 26
camel(s) 52, 146
camelids 43, 50, 51
Canada 59, 155
Canadian 60
cannibalism 142
canoe(s) 135, 136, 138, 139
Canoe Indians 103, 134
Cape Desire 114
Cape Horn 27, 32, 33, 36,
    39, 52, 99, 100, 102-104,
    107, 108, 110, 168
Cape Horn Current 50
Cape of Desire 95

Cape of Good Hope
    32, 90, 110, 112
Cape of the Eleven Thousand
    Virgins 92, 98, 160
Caracara 19, 82
Cassidy, Butch 165
cat 43
cattle 15, 24, 27, 57, 79
Cavendish, Thomas 106
caves 166
CCAS 68
cephalopods 69
Charles I, King of Spain 90
charqui 55
Chile 2, 4, 9, 23-26, 28, 40,
    41, 46, 47, 49, 51-53,
    74, 76 85, 127, 151-
    158, 162, 163, 166, 167
Chilean Naval Base 3, 31
Chouinard, Yvon 163, 164
Christian 120, 123
Christian Democrat(s) 152,
    154
chulengos 18, 51, 54
ciexaus 136
CITES 53, 68, 73
cloves 95
coal 151
coigue 86
Cold War 157
Coleridge, Samuel 104, 107,
    108
Communion 98
Communists, 152
concentration camp 158, 159
Condor Bay 6, 111
Condor Mountain 8
Conway, William, 52
Cook, James 102-104, 109,
    140, 142
copper 152
cordilleran region 46

Cordon de los Dientes 31
cormorant(s) 14, 80
coscoroba swan 19, 83
cowboy 133
crayfish 24
crevasses 5, 45
Croatian 15
Croatian immigrants 30
Cruceros Australis 2
crustaceans 69, 75
Cuernos del Paine 42
Cueva de las Manos (Cave of
    the Hands) 166
cybercafes 31

D

Dana, RichardHenry 33
Dante 113
Darwin, Charles 23, 36, 40
    103, 105, 106, 115, 119,
    124, 137, 142, 146
Darwin Range 11
Davis, John 106
Dawson Island 158, 159
De Solis 91
deer 52, 132
dinosaur eggs 165
disease(s) 137, 147
dolphins 62
Dominican gull 75
Don Manoel, King of Portu-
    gal, 90
"doubling the Horn" 32
Doughty, John 98
Drake 84, 97-100, 168
Drake Strait 32, 33, 102,
    112
dung 43
Dutch 101, 107, 112,
    114, 140
Dutch East India Company
    101

E

eagles 59
East Indies 101
electronic firms 25
electronics 160
elephant seals 4
England 27, 97, 99, 100,
    116, 120, 121, 123, 124
English Channel 135
English Queen 99
equator 52
Escobar, RicardoLagos 154
Eskimo-English dictionary
    136
Esprit 163
estancia 15
Europe 27, 55, 119, 167
European Community 60
explorers 140

F

Falkland Islands 118, 119,
    121, 125, 150, 158, 166
Ferdinand 152
Firelanders 130
firn 44
First National Bank 165
fish 24, 63, 65, 69,
    75, 159, 160
fishing 10, 27
FitzRoy, CaptainRobert
    111, 122-125,137
Five Pyramids 8
fjord(s) 6, 22, 151
flamingo(s) 15, 82
Flightless Steamer Duck 83
flying steamer duck 84
forest products 159
forestry-related industries 27
fox(es) 57, 59
Frei-Montalva, Eduardo 152

French 140
French frigate, 109
French Revolution 26
Frenchwoman 109
Fuegia Basket 123, 124
Fuegian(s) 103, 123- 125, 130
fur seal(s) 67, 69
furniture manufacturing 10

G

Gabriel Channel 14
Galapagos Islands 106
Gardiner, Allen 115-118, 150
Garibaldi Glacier 12
Garibaldi Sound 13
gas 159
gaucho 133
geese 84
German(s) 145, 157
German Catholic priest 31
giant petrel 75
giants 113, 129
glacial ice crystals 5
glacier(s) 4-6, 8, 12, 13, 15, 21, 22, 42, 44, 45, 48, 111, 165
glacier ice drinks 13
glaciologists 22
global warming 5, 21
goats 151
gold 24, 30, 112, 160, 161
gold panners 147
Golden Age of Sail 32
Golden Hind 98
Gondwana 166
Gospel 116
granite 42
greater rhea 79
grebes 84
Greenpeace 162
grey fox(es) 19, 58

Grey Glacier 18
guanaco 8, 15, 17, 18, 31, 43, 50-55, 57, 58, 128, 129, 132, 133
guanaco wool 55
Gulf war 150

H

hain 132
Halakwulup 134
Hard Rock Café 164
harpoons 136, 139
Haush 103, 130, 142
hawks 84
Holland 100
Holy Orders 121
Hoorn 101, 102
Horn 109, 112
horse(s) 8, 43, 52, 54, 104, 130
Hoste 40
Hosterîa Rîo Verde, 20
hotel(s) 158, 164
huemel 56, 57
Huilliche 128
Humboldt Current 49
Hungarians 145
Huns 92

I

Ibañez, Don Gegorio 160
ice 5, 13
ice fields 21, 44
ice floes 4, 6, 18
immigrants 27
India 90
Indian Oceans 99
International Expeditions 11, 65, 98
International Whaling Commission 63

Internet 31
Iquique 155
IsaacLeMair e 101
Isla Desolación 46
Isla Gordon 40
Isla Grande 23, 46
Isla Magdalena 98
Isla Navarino 31
Isthmus of Panama 58, 112
Italian 91, 149

J

Jemmy Button 122-126
Juan Perón 150
junta 151

K

Kawéskar 134
Kayakers 49
kelp 135
kelp geese 14
kelp gulls 13, 81
King, CaptainParker 1 10
King Cormorants 80
king crab 30
King George Island, Antarctica. 155
King's treasurer 92
krill 25, 66, 68
Kris McDivitt 164

L

La Primavera (Springtime) 164
laissez-faire economic policies 153
Lake District 127
Lake Grey 18
Las Minas creek 160
las pampas 24
Latin America 155

Le Prince 109
Lecaros, DonPedr o 2
lenga 85, 86, 161, 162
Lennox 40, 419
Lesser rheas 17, 19, 76-79, 132
Lewis, Charlie 164
Lima 116
limestone 151
liquor 147
Lisbon 90
livestock 30
llama 50, 51
London 43
lupine 12, 86

M

machine repair shops 27
Magallanes region 2, 28
Magdalena Island 15, 75, 76
Magellan 24, 39, 51, 89-95, 97, 98, 100, 106, 112-114, 130, 144, 145, 168
Magellanic penguins 14, 16, 74
Malvinas 166
Manantiales 24
Manchester 47, 48
Mannenkenk 130
Mapuche 128
Marinelli Glacier 3
Maritime Government of Tierra del Fuego 10
Marshall, James 160
massacre 119, 126
Maximilian Transylvanus 146
Mediterranean 97
Melville 102, 113
mesquite 15
mesquite-like shrub 86
Mexico 112, 157
Milodon Cave 19, 43

Minister of Defense 154
Mirador el Payne 17
missionary(ies) 119, 121,
    119, 131, 137, 146, 147
Mississippi River 2
mollusks 25
Moluccas 90, 101
Monte Darwin 23
Monte Sarmiento 23
moraines 22, 24
Morocco 90
Morris 104
mule 52
Murray Narrows 137
Museo del Fin del Mundo 11
Museo del Recuerdo 28
Museo Martin Gusinde 31
Museo Salesiano 1, 27
museum 9, 136
mussels 25, 138
mutton 27

N

NAFTA 155
Napoleon's brother Joseph
    151
Narborough, CaptainJohn
    107, 114
narwhal 101, 102
Native Americans 136
natural gas 151, 158
Naval Chapel 9, 31
Navarino Island 40, 83, 121
Navy, 116
New Guinea 116
New Hampshire 23
New Zealand 32
ñirre 86
North America 32, 55, 127,
    167
Northern elephant seal 65
Northern hemisphere 47

Nueva 40, 41
nutria 24

O

O'Higgins, Bernardo, 152
oil 27, 30, 158, 159
Ona(s) 54, 55, 130-134,
    140
Orca 62
ornithologist(s) 6, 16
Orundellico 123
ostriches 76
otter-skin 135
oxen 29
ozone depletion 30

P

Paachek 133
Pacific 23, 32, 36, 40, 47,
    95, 98-101, 107, 110,
    112
pampas 17, 133, 168
Panama Canal 27, 32
passports 9
Patagones Strait 95
Patagonia Missionary Society
    116, 125
Patagonian Cavy 61
Patagonian Indians 119
Patagonian Institute 28
Patagonian Islands. 14
Paul Theroux' 12
Peaceful Sea 94
Peat moss 87
Pehuenche, 128
Pelican 98
penguin(s) 14, 16, 63, 65, 69,
    74, 98
penguin rookery 75
Pernette, Jean-Francois 166
Peru 50, 51, 76, 100,

112, 116, 157
petroleum reserves 151
Philippines 95
Pia Fjord 12
Pia Glacier 12, 13
Picton 40, 41, 116
Piedra Buena 150, 151
Pigafetta, Antonio 51, 91,
    94,-97, 106, 113, 114,
    144, 145
Pinochet, GeneralAugusto
    41, 153, 155, 158, 159,
    162
Pinto River 17
Planet Hollywood 164
plastics 160
platypus tooth 165, 166
plebiscite 153
Pleistocene 21
Poe 113
Porter, CaptainDavid 1 10
Portugal 27
Portuguese 90, 97
Porvenir 14, 15, 24, 25,
    30, 82, 161
power plants 158
pre-English 124
Primera Angostura 22
prison(s) 9-12, 26, 29,
    158, 159
prisoner(s) 26, 29
prostitutes 26
Puelche 128
Puerto Español 150
Puerto Montt 155
Puerto Natales 19, 20, 43, 83
Puerto Williams
    3, 7, 9, 25, 31, 32, 49,
    83
puma(s) 51, 56, 57
Punta Arenas 1-3, 7, 8,
    15, 16, 20, 25-27,

40, 47, 48, 136, 155,
    158, 159, 160, 161
Pythagoras 112

Q

Queen 98
quillango 54

R

Radicals, 152
railroad 11, 12, 30
Reconquista 152
red deer 56
red fox, 58
Redskins 131
Rhode Island 163
right whale(s) 64, 65
Río Condor project 161, 162
Río de la Plata 91
Río Gallegos 24
Río Grande 24, 25, 46,
    158
Río Negro 128
Rock Cormorants 80
rodents 60
roots 132
Royal Navy 115
Ruiz-Tagle, EduardoFr ei 154
Russia 27
Russian ship 9

S

sailboat 7
Salesian missionaries 159
salinity 49
Salto Grande 17
San Francisco 27, 99
San Julian 92
Santiago 2, 20, 47, 155, 156
Sarmiento, DonPedr o 100
sauropod 165

Savannah, 2
sawmill(s) 27, 29
Schouten, Wilhelm Cornelius
    100- 102
scientific research station 30
scurvy 118
sea lion(s) 13, 14, 63, 70, 138
Sea Madonna 31
seafood. 151
sealers 146, 147
seal(s) 24, 63, 137, 138
seaweed 135
Segunda Angostura. 22
Selk'nam 130
Serrano Glacier 6
Shakespeare 136
sheep 15, 20, 24, 27, 52,
    54, 57, 79, 133, 147,
    151, 159
sheep farmers 147
Sheep raising 10
shipwreck 160
Siberia 127
silver 112
ski areas 10
sledge homes 10
sloth 20, 43, 44
Snow, Captain William 125
Socialist Party, 152
Socialists 152
soldiers 26
Soros, George 164, 165
South Africa 64
South America 23, 39, 49
    51, 52, 55, 74, 76,
    107, 112, 145, 157, 165-
    167
south Atlantic 91, 109
South Georgia Islands 104
South Sea 90, 94
Southern Elephant Seal 65
Southern Fur Seal 66, 68

Southern hemisphere 47
Southern Right Whale 63
Southern Sea Lion(s) 68,
    69, 71, 75
Spain 27, 90, 91, 94-96,
    112
Spanish Viceroy 100
spears 139
spider crabs 25
Spilbergen, Admiral 114
squid(s) 63, 65, 66, 75
St. Julian 93, 98
St. Ursula 92
Stallone, Sylvester 165
Staten Island 151, 166
Stewart Island 32
Strait of Magellan 3, 22-
    25, 27, 32,
    39, 41, 47, 90, 92,
    94-96, 98, 100-102,
    106, 107, 109, 128,
    130, 131, 151, 152,
    160
Sundance Kid 165
Supreme Court. 154
Sutter's Creek, California 160
Switzerland 27
syphilis 147

T

Tehuelche(s) 26, 54, 114,
    128-131, 140, 144,
    168
Tennyson 113
Terminal moraines 22
Terra Australis 2, 6, 13,
    39, 49, 111
textile(s) 25, 160
tides 49
Tierra del Fuego 3, 10,
    15, 22-25, 28, 30,

39-41, 46, 47, 49,
50, 53, 55, 59, 61,
81, 83, 85-87, 92,
100, 103, 110, 116, 118,
120, 121, 124, 125, 127,
130, 131, 133, 151, 158,
161, 162
Tierra del Fuego National
Park 9, 11, 12, 30, 87
timber 24
Todos los Santos 95
Tompkins, Doug 163, 164
Torres del Paine National
Park 16, 17, 19, 42, 49,
52, 53, 57, 82,
83, 85, 168
tourism 10, 27, 158
Trillium Corporation 161, 162
Tucker Island 14
turkey vulture(s) 14, 81
Turner, Ted 164
tussock grass 24

U

U.S. 150, 152, 163
UNESCO Biosphere Reserve.
42
United States 27, 42, 51,
155, 157, 167
Unity 101, 102
University of Magellanes 2
US Navy 110
Ushuaia 3, 9-12, 24, 25,
28-30, 46, 83, 121, 122,
131, 133, 158, 162

V

Valdivia 2
Valparaiso 155
Vatican 41
Venezuela 72

Vermont 23
vicuna 50, 51
Vittoria 95
volcanic eruption. 99
volcanoes 156

W

Wales 51
War of 1812 110
Watawuinewua 137
waterfall(s) 8, 42
Weddell, James 146
western hemisphere 56
whale(s) 14, 24, 25, 63,
64, 137
wild celery, 132
williwaw(s) 17, 40, 47, 48
Winnemucca, Nevada 165
Wolische 129
wolves 59
wooden "railway" 29
wool 27, 51, 53, 129

Y

Yaghan(s) 28, 31, 103,
118, 119, 121-123,
130, 131, 133-137,
139, 140, 142
Yaghan-English dictionary.
121
Yahgashagalumoala 137
Yamana 134, 137
Yendegaia Bay 8
Yendegaia Ranch 7
York Minister 123-125
Yosemite National Park 42
Yugoslavia 27

Z

zodiac(s) 3, 13, 14
Zululand 116

ORDER FORM

INTERNATIONAL EXPEDITIONS

Name_____

Address_____

City/State/Zip_____

Phone(H)_____(W)_____

❏ I want information about the Patagonia
trip described in this book.

❏ I want information about the other trips
conducted by International Expeditions.

INTERNATIONAL EXPEDITIONS
One Environs Park
Helena, Alabama 35080

Call toll-free at 800-633-4734

FAX 205-428-1714

Website:
http://www.internationalexpeditions.com

ORDER FORM

DIMI PRESS

Name_____

Address_____

City/State/Zip_____

Phone_____

Enclosed is my check for $22.45 ($18.95 for *PATAGONIA* and $3.50 for shipping) or:

Credit card:_____
(Visa or MC accepted)

Expiration date:_____

DIMI PRESS
3820 Oak Hollow Lane. SE
Salem, OR 97302-4774

Call toll-free: 800-644-DIMI(3464) for orders
Phone: 503-364-7698 for information
FAX:503-364-9727
E-mail: dickbook@earthlink.net
Web: http://home.earthlink.net/~dickbook